THE BLACK (

by
Cyril McNeile ("Sapper")

First Published 1922
Republished 2023

CONTENTS

1. In which things happen near Barking Creek
2. In which Scotland Yard sits up and takes notice
3. In which Hugh Drummond composes a letter
4. In which Count Zadowa gets a shock
5. In which Charles Latter, M.P., goes mad
6. In which an effusion is sent to the newspapers
7. In which a bomb bursts at unpleasantly close quarters
8. In which the bag of nuts is found by accident
9. In which there is a stormy supper party at the Ritz
10. In which Hugh Drummond makes a discovery
11. In which Hugh Drummond and the Reverend Theodosius Longmoor take lunch together
12. In which Count Zadowa is introduced to "Alice in Wonderland"
13. In which Hugh Drummond and the Reverend Theodosius have a little chat
14. In which a Rolls-Royce runs amok
15. In which Hugh Drummond arrives at Maybrick Hall
16. In which things happen at Maybrick Hall
17. In which a murderer is murdered at Maybrick Hall
18. In which the Home Secretary is taught the Fox-trot

1

In which things happen
near Barking Creek

The wind howled dismally round a house standing by itself almost on the shores of Barking Creek. It was the grey dusk of an early autumn day, and the occasional harsh cry of a sea-gull rising discordantly above the wind alone broke the silence of the flat, desolate waste.

The house seemed deserted. Every window was shuttered; the garden was uncared for and a mass of weeds; the gate leading on to the road, apparently feeling the need of a deficient top hinge, propped itself drunkenly on what had once been a flower-bed. A few gloomy trees swaying dismally in the wind surrounded the house and completed the picture—one that would have caused even the least imaginative of men to draw his coat a little tighter round him, and feel thankful that it was not his fate to live in such a place.

But then few people ever came near enough to the house to realize its sinister appearance. The road—it was little better than a cart track—which passed the gate, was out of the beaten way; only an occasional fisherman or farm labourer ever used it, and that generally by day when things assumed their proper proportion, and it was merely an empty house gradually falling to pieces through lack of attention. At night they avoided it if possible; folks did say that twelve years ago some prying explorer had found the bones of a skeleton lying on the floor in one of the upstairs rooms with a mildewed rope fixed to one of the beams in the ceiling. And then it had been empty for twenty years.

Even now when the wind lay in the east or north-east and the tide was setting in, there were those who said that you could see a light shining through the cracks in the shutters in that room upstairs, and that, should a man climb up and look in, he'd see no skeleton, but a body with purple face and staring eyes swinging gently to and fro, and tied by the neck to a beam with a rope which showed no trace of mildew. Ridiculous, of course; but then so many of these local superstitions are. Useful, too, in some cases; they afford a privacy from the prying attention of local gossips far more cheaply and effectively than high walls and bolts and bars.

So, at any rate, one of the two men who were walking briskly along the rough track seemed to think.

"Admirable," he remarked, as he paused for a moment at the entrance of the weed-grown drive. "Quite admirable, my friend. A house situated as this one is, is an acquisition, and when it is haunted in addition it becomes a godsend."

He spoke English perfectly with a slight foreign accent, and his companion nodded abruptly.

"From what I heard about it, I thought it would do," he answered. "Personally I think it's a damnable spot, but since you were so set against coming to London, I had to find somewhere in this neighbourhood."

The two men started to walk slowly up the drive. Branches dripping with moisture brushed across their faces, and involuntarily they both turned up the collars of their coats.

"I will explain my reasons in due course," said the first speaker shortly. "You may take it from me that they were good. What's that?"

He swung round with a little gasp, clutching his companion's arm.

"Nothing," cried the other irritably. For a moment or two they stood still, peering into the dark undergrowth. "What did you think it was?"

"I thought I heard a bush creaking as if—as if someone was moving," he said, relaxing his grip. "It must have been the wind, I suppose."

He still peered fearfully into the gloomy garden, until the other man dragged him roughly towards the house.

"Of course it was the wind," he muttered angrily. "For heaven's sake, Zaboleff, don't get the jumps. If you will insist on coming to an infernal place like this to transact a little perfectly normal business you must expect a few strange noises and sounds. Let's get indoors; the others should be here by now. It oughtn't to take more than an hour, and you can be on board again long before dawn."

The man who had been addressed as Zaboleff ceased looking over his shoulder, and followed the other through a broken-down lattice-gate to the rear of the house. They paused in front of the back door, and on it the leader knocked three times in a peculiar way. It was obviously a pre-arranged signal, for almost at once stealthy steps could be heard coming along the passage inside. The door was cautiously pulled back a few inches, and a man peered out, only to throw it open wide with a faint sigh of relief.

"It's you, Mr. Waldock, is it?" he muttered. "Glad you've got 'ere at last. This place is fair giving us all the 'ump."

"Evening, Jim." He stepped inside, followed by Zaboleff, and the door closed behind them. "Our friend's boat was a little late. Is everyone here?"

"Yep," answered the other. "All the six of us. And I reckons we'd like to get it over as soon as possible. Has he"—his voice sank to a hoarse undertone—"has he brought the money?"

"You'll all hear in good time," said Waldock curtly. "Which is the room?"

"'Ere it is, guv'nor." Jim flung open a door. "And you'll 'ave to sit on the floor, as the chairs ain't safe."

Two candles guttered on a square table in the centre of the room, showing up the faces of the five men who sat on the floor, leaning against the walls. Three of them were nondescript specimens of humanity of the type that may be seen by the thousand hurrying into the City by the early business trains. They were representative of the poorer type of clerk—the type which Woodbines its fingers to a brilliant orange; the type that screams insults at a football referee on Saturday afternoon. And yet to the close observer something more might be read on their faces: a greedy, hungry look, a shifty, untrustworthy look—the look of those who are jealous of everyone better placed than themselves, but who are incapable of trying to better their own position except by the relative method of dragging back their more fortunate acquaintances; the look of little men dissatisfied not so much with their own littleness as with the bigness of other people. A nasty-faced trio with that smattering of education which is the truly dangerous thing; and—three of Mr. Waldock's clerks.

The two others were Jews; a little flashily dressed, distinctly addicted to cheap jewellery. They were sitting apart from the other three, talking in low tones, but as the door opened, their conversation ceased abruptly and they looked up at the new-comers with the keen, searching look of their race. Waldock they hardly glanced at; it was the stranger Zaboleff who riveted their attention. They took in every detail of the shrewd, foreign face—the olive skin, the dark, piercing eyes, the fine-pointed beard; they measured him up as a boxer measures up his opponent, or a business man takes stock of the second party in a deal; then once again they conversed together in low tones which were barely above a whisper.

It was Jim who broke the silence—Flash Jim, to give him the full name to which he answered in the haunts he frequented.

"Wot abaht getting on with it, guv'nor?" he remarked with an attempt at a genial smile. "This 'ere 'ouse ain't wot I'd choose for a blooming 'oneymoon."

With an abrupt gesture Waldock silenced him and advanced to the table.

"This is Mr. Zaboleff, gentlemen," he said quietly. "We are a little late, I am afraid, but it was unavoidable. He will explain to you now the reason why you were asked to come here, and not meet at our usual rendezvous in Soho."

He stepped back a couple of paces and Zaboleff took his place. For a moment or two he glanced round at the faces turned expectantly towards him; then resting his two hands on the table in front of him, he leaned forward towards them.

"Gentlemen," he began, and the foreign accent seemed a little more pronounced, "I have asked you to come here to-night through my good friend, Mr. Waldock, because it has come to our ears—no matter how—that London is no longer a safe meeting-place. Two or three things have occurred lately the significance of which it is impossible to disregard."

"Wot sort of things?" interrupted Flash Jim harshly.

"I was about to tell you," remarked the speaker suavely, and Flash Jim subsided, abashed. "Our chief, with whom I spent last evening, is seriously concerned about these things."

"You spent last night with the chief?" said Waldock, and his voice held a tremour of excitement, while the others leaned forward eagerly. "Is he, then, in Holland?"

"He was at six o'clock yesterday evening," answered Zaboleff with a faint smile. "To-day—now—I know no more than you where he is."

"Who is he—this man we're always hearing about and never seeing?" demanded one of the three clerks aggressively.

"He is—the Chief," replied the other, while his eyes seemed to bore into the speaker's brain. "Just that—and no more. And that is quite enough for you." His glance travelled round the room, and his audience relaxed. "By the way, is not that a chink in the shutter there?"

"All the safer," grunted Flash Jim. "Anyone passing will think the ghost is walking."

"Nevertheless, kindly cover it up," ordered Zaboleff, and one of the Jews rose and wedged his pocket-handkerchief into the crack. There was silence in the room while he did so, a silence broken only by the mournful hooting of an owl outside.

"Owls is the only things wot comes to this damned museum," said Flash Jim morosely. "Owls and blinking fools like us."

"Stow it, Jim," snarled Waldock furiously. "Anyone would think you wanted a nurse."

"Gentlemen—please." Zaboleff held up a protesting hand. "We do not want to prolong matters, but one or two explanations are necessary. To return, then, to these things that have happened recently, and which necessitated a fresh rendezvous for this evening—one which our friend Mr. Waldock so obligingly found. Three messengers sent over during the last three weeks bearing instructions and—what is more important—money, have disappeared."

"Disappeared?" echoed Waldock stupidly.

"Absolutely and completely. Money and all. Two more have been abominably illtreated and had their money taken from them, but for some reason they were allowed to go free themselves. It is from them that we have obtained our information."

"Blimey!" muttered Flash Jim; "is it the police?"

"It is not the police, which is what makes it so much more serious," answered Zaboleff quietly, and Flash Jim breathed a sigh of relief. "It is easy to keep within the law, but if our information is correct we are up against a body of men who are not within the law themselves. A body of men who are absolutely unscrupulous and utterly ruthless; a body of men who appear to know our secret plans as well as we do ourselves. And the difficulty of it is, gentlemen, that though, legally speaking, on account of the absurd legislation in this country we may keep within the law ourselves, we are hardly in a position to appeal to the police for protection. Our activities, though allowed officially, are hardly such as would appeal even to the English authorities. And on this occasion particularly that is the case. You may remember that the part I played in stirring up bloodshed at Cowdenheath a few months ago, under the name of MacTavish, caused me to be deported. So though our cause is legal—my presence in this country is not. Which was why to-night it was particularly essential that we should not be disturbed. Not only are we all up against this unknown gang of men, but I, in addition, am up against the police."

"Have you any information with regard to this gang?" It was the Jew who had closed the chink in the shutters speaking for the first time.

"None of any use—save that they are masked in black, and cloaked in long black cloaks." He paused a moment as if to collect his thoughts. "They are all armed, and Petrovitch—he was one of the men allowed to escape—was very insistent on one point. It concerned the leader of the gang, whom he affirmed was a man of the most gigantic physical strength; a giant powerful as two ordinary strong men. He said, ... Ach! Mein Gott——!"

His voice rose to a scream as he cowered back, while the others, with terror on their faces, rose hurriedly from their seats on the floor and huddled together in the corners of the room.

In the doorway stood a huge man covered from head to foot in black. In each hand he held a revolver, with which he covered the eight occupants during the second or two which it took for half a dozen similarly disguised men to file past him, and take up their positions round the walls. And Waldock, a little more educated than the remainder of his friends, found himself thinking of old tales of the Spanish Inquisition and the Doges of Venice even as he huddled a little nearer to the table.

"Stand by the table, all of you."

It was the man at the door who spoke in a curiously deep voice, and like sheep they obeyed him—all save Flash Jim. For that worthy, crook though he was, was not without physical courage. The police he knew better than to play the fool with, but these were not the police.

"Wot the——" he snarled, and got no further.

Something hit him behind the head, a thousand stars danced before his eyes, and with a strangled grunt he crashed forward on his face.

For a moment or two there was silence, and then once again the man at the door spoke.

"Arrange the specimens in a row."

In a second the seven remaining men were marshalled in a line, while behind them stood six motionless black figures. And then the big man walked slowly down in front of them, peering into each man's face. He spoke no word until he reached the end of the line, and then, his inspection concluded, he stepped back and leaned against the wall facing them.

"A nauseating collection," he remarked thoughtfully. "A loathsome brood. What are the three undersized and shivering insects on the right?"

"Those are three of my clerks," said Waldock with an assumption of angry bravado. "And I would like to know——"

"In good time you will," answered the deep voice. "Three of your clerks, are they; imbued with your rotten ideas, I suppose, and yearning to follow in father's footsteps? Have we anything particular against them?"

There was no answer from the masked men, and the leader made a sign. Instantly the three terrified clerks were seized from behind and brought up to him, where they stood trembling and shaking in every limb.

"Listen to me, you three little worms." With an effort they pulled themselves together; a ray of hope was dawning in their minds—perhaps they were going to be let off easy. "My friends and I do not like you or your type. You meet in secret places and in your slimy minds you concoct foul schemes which, incredible though it may seem, have so far had more than a fair measure of success in this country. But your main idea is not the schemes, but the money you are paid to carry them out. This is your first and last warning. Another time you will be treated differently. Get out of here. And see you don't stop."

The door closed behind them and two of the masked men; there was the sound as of a boot being used with skill and strength, and cries of pain; then the door reopened and the masked men returned.

"They are gone," announced one of them. "We helped them on their way."

"Good," said the leader. "Let us continue the inspection. What are these two Hebrews?"

A man from behind stepped forward and examined them slowly; then he came up to the leader and whispered in his ear.

"Is that so?" A new and terrible note had crept into the deep voice. "My friends and I do not like your trade, you swine. It is well that we have come provided with the necessary implement for such a case. Fetch the cat."

In silence one of the men left the room, and as his full meaning came home to the two Jews they flung themselves grovelling on the floor, screaming for mercy.

"Gag them."

The order came out sharp and clear, and in an instant the two writhing men were seized and gagged. Only their rolling eyes and trembling hands showed the terror they felt as they dragged themselves on their knees towards the impassive leader.

"The cat for cases of this sort is used legally," he remarked. "We merely anticipate the law."

With a fresh outburst of moans the two Jews watched the door open and the inexorable black figure come in, holding in his hand a short stick from which nine lashes hung down.

"Heavens!" gasped Waldock, starting forward. "What are you going to do?"

"Flog them to within an inch of their lives," said the deep voice. "It is the punishment for their method of livelihood. Five and six—take charge. After you have finished remove them in Number 3 car, and drop them in London."

Struggling impotently, the Jews were led away, and the leader passed on to the remaining two men.

"So, Zaboleff, you came after all. Unwise, surely, in view of the police?"

"Who are you?" muttered Zaboleff, his lips trembling.

"A specimen hunter," said the other suavely. "I am making a collection of people like you. The police of our country are unduly kind to your breed, although they would not have been kind to you to-night, Zaboleff, unless I had intervened. But I couldn't let them have you; you're such a very choice

8

specimen. I don't think somehow that you've worked this little flying visit of yours very well. Of course I knew about it, but I must confess I was surprised when I found that the police did too."

"What do you mean?" demanded the other hoarsely.

"I mean that when we arrived here we found to our surprise that the police had forestalled us. Popular house, this, to-night."

"The police!" muttered Waldock dazedly.

"Even so—led by no less a personage than Inspector McIver. They had completely surrounded the house, and necessitated a slight change in my plans."

"Where are they now?" cried Waldock.

"Ah! Where indeed? Let us trust at any rate in comfort."

"By heaven!" said Zaboleff, taking a step forward. "As I asked you before—who are you?"

"And as I told you before, Zaboleff, a collector of specimens. Some I keep; some I let go—as you have already seen."

"And what are you going to do with me?"

"Keep you. Up to date you are the cream of my collection."

"Are you working with the police?" said the other dazedly.

"Until to-night we have not clashed. Even to-night, well, I think we are working towards the same end. And do you know what that end is, Zaboleff?" The deep voice grew a little sterner. "It is the utter, final overthrow of you and all that you stand for. To achieve that object we shall show no mercy. Even as you are working in the dark—so are we. Already you are frightened; already we have proved that you fear the unknown more than you fear the police; already the first few tricks are ours. But you still hold the ace, Zaboleff—or shall we say the King of Trumps? And when we catch him you will cease to be the cream of my collection. This leader of yours—it was what Petrovitch told him, I suppose, that made him send you over."

"I refuse to say," said the other.

"You needn't; it is obvious. And now that you are caught—he will come himself. Perhaps not at once—but he will come. And then.... But we waste time. The money, Zaboleff."

"I have no money," he snarled.

"You lie, Zaboleff. You lie clumsily. You have quite a lot of money brought over for Waldock so that he might carry on the good work after you had sailed! to-morrow. Quick, please; time passes."

With a curse Zaboleff produced a small canvas bag and held it out. The other took it and glanced inside.

"I see," he said gravely. "Pearls and precious stones. Belonging once, I suppose, to a murdered gentlewoman whose only crime was that she, through no action of her own, was born in a different sphere to you. And, you reptile"—his voice rose a little—"you would do that here."

Zaboleff shrank back, and the other laughed contemptuously.

"Search him—and Waldock too."

9

Two men stepped forward quickly.

"Nothing more," they said after a while. "Except this piece of paper."

There was a sudden movement on Zaboleff's part—instantly suppressed, but not quite soon enough.

"Injudicious," said the leader quietly. "Memory is better. An address, I see—No. 5, Green Street, Hoxton. A salubrious neighbourhood, with which I am but indifferently acquainted. Ah! I see my violent friend has recovered." He glanced at Flash Jim, who was sitting up dazedly, rubbing the back of his head. "Number 4, the usual."

There was a slight struggle, and Flash Jim lay back peacefully unconscious, while a faint smell of chloroform filled the room.

"And now I think we will go. A most successful evening."

"What are you going to do with me, you scoundrel?" spluttered Waldock. "I warn you that I have influential friends, who—who will ask questions in—in Parliament if you do anything to me; who will go to Scotland Yard."

"I can assure you, Mr. Waldock, that I will make it my personal business to see that their natural curiosity is gratified," answered the leader suavely. "But for the present I fear the three filthy rags you edit will have to be content with the office boy as their guiding light. And I venture to think they will not suffer."

He made a sudden sign, and before they realized what was happening the two men were caught from behind and gagged. The next instant they were rushed through the door, followed by Flash Jim. For a moment or two the eyes of the leader wandered round the now empty room taking in every detail: then he stepped forward and blew out the two candles. The door closed gently behind him, and a couple of minutes later two cars stole quietly away from the broken-down gate along the cart track. It was just midnight; behind them the gloomy house stood up gaunt and forbidding against the darkness of the night sky. And it was not until the leading car turned carefully into the main road that anyone spoke.

"Deuced awkward, the police being there."

The big man who was driving grunted thoughtfully.

"Perhaps," he returned. "Perhaps not. Anyway, the more the merrier. Flash Jim all right?"

"Sleeping like a child," answered the other, peering into the body of the car.

For about ten miles they drove on in silence: then at a main cross-roads the car pulled up and the big man got out. The second car was just behind, and for a few moments there was a whispered conversation between him and the other driver. He glanced at Zaboleff and Waldock, who appeared to be peacefully sleeping on the back seat, and smiled grimly.

"Good night, old man. Report as usual."

"Right," answered the driver. "So long."

The second car swung right-handed and started northwards, while the leader stood watching the vanishing tail lamp. Then he returned to his own seat, and soon the first beginnings of outer London were reached. And it was as they reached Whitechapel that the leader spoke again with a note of suppressed excitement in his voice.

"We're worrying 'em; we're worrying 'em badly. Otherwise they'd never have sent Zaboleff. He was too big a man to risk, considering the police."

"It's the police that I *am* considering," said his companion.

The big man laughed.

"Leave that to me, old man; leave that entirely to me."

2

In which Scotland Yard sits up and takes notice

Sir Bryan Johnstone leaned back in his chair and stared at the ceiling with a frown. His hands were thrust deep into his trouser pockets; his long legs were stretched out to their full extent under the big roll-top desk in front of him. From the next room came the monotonous tapping of a typewriter, and after a while Sir Bryan closed his eyes.

Through the open window there came the murmur of the London traffic—that soothing sound so conducive to sleep in those who have lunched well. But that did not apply to the man lying back in his chair. Sir Bryan's lunch was always a frugal meal, and it was no desire for sleep that made the Director of Criminal Investigation close his eyes. He was puzzled, and the report lying on the desk in front of him was the reason.

For perhaps ten minutes he remained motionless, then he leaned forward and touched an electric bell. Instantly the typewriter ceased, and a girl secretary came quickly into the room.

"Miss Forbes," said Sir Bryan, "I wish you would find out if Chief Inspector McIver is in the building. If so I would like to see him at once; if not, see that he gets the message as soon as he comes in."

The door closed behind the girl, and after a moment or two the man rose from his desk and began to pace up and down the room with long, even strides. Every now and then he would stop and stare at some print on the wall, but it was the blank stare of a man whose mind is engrossed in other matters.

And once while he stood looking out of the window, he voiced his thoughts, unconscious that he spoke aloud.

"Dash it, McIver's not fanciful. He's the least fanciful man we've got. And yet..."

His eyes came round to the desk once more, the desk on which the report was lying. It was Inspector McIver's report—hence his instructions to the secretary. It was the report on a very strange matter which had taken place the previous night, and after a while Sir Bryan picked up the typed sheets and

11

glanced through them again. And he was still standing by the desk, idly turning over the pages when the secretary came into the room.

"Chief Inspector McIver is here, Sir Bryan," she announced.

"Tell him to come in, Miss Forbes."

Certainly the Inspector justified his Chief's spoken thought—a less fanciful looking man it would have been hard to imagine. A square-jawed, rugged Scotchman, he looked the type to whom Holy Writ was Holy Writ only in so far as it could be proved. He was short and thick-set, and his physical strength was proverbial. But a pair of kindly twinkling eyes belied the gruff voice. In fact, the gruff voice was a pose specially put on which deceived no one; his children all imitated it to his huge content, though he endeavoured to look ferocious when they did so. In short, McIver, though shrewd and relentless when on duty, was the kindest-hearted of men. But he was most certainly not fanciful.

"What the dickens is all this about, McIver," said Sir Bryan with a smile, when the door had shut behind the secretary.

"I wish I knew myself, sir," returned the other seriously. "I've never been so completely defeated in my life."

Sir Bryan waved him to a chair and sat down at the desk.

"I've read your report," he said, still smiling, "and frankly, McIver, if it had been anyone but you, I should have been annoyed. But I know you far too well for that. Look here"—he pushed a box of cigarettes across the table—"take a cigarette and your time and let's hear about it."

McIver lit a cigarette and seemed to be marshalling his thoughts. He was a man who liked to tell his story in his own way, and his chief waited patiently till he was ready. He knew that when his subordinate did start he would get a clear, concise account of what had taken place, with everything irrelevant ruthlessly cut out. And if there was one thing that roused Sir Bryan to thoughts of murder and violence, it was a rambling, incoherent statement from one of his men.

"Well, sir," began McIver at length, "this is briefly what took place. At ten o'clock last night as we had arranged, we completely surrounded the suspected house on the outskirts of Barking. I had had a couple of good men on duty there lying concealed the whole day, and when I arrived at about nine-thirty with Sergeant Andrews and half-a-dozen others, they reported to me that at least eight men were inside, and that Zaboleff was one of them. He had been shadowed the whole way down from Limehouse with another man, and both the watchers were positive that he had not left the house. So I posted my men and crept forward to investigate myself. There was a little chink in the wooden shutters of one of the downstairs rooms through which the light was streaming. I took a glimpse through, and found that everything was just as had been reported to me. There were eight of them there, and an unpleasant-looking bunch they were, too. Zaboleff I saw at the head of the table, and standing next to him was that man Waldock who runs two or three of the worst of the Red papers. There was also Flash Jim, and I began to wish I'd brought a few more men."

McIver smiled ruefully. "It was about the last coherent wish I remember. And," he went on seriously, "what I'm going to tell you now, sir, may seem extraordinary and what one would expect in detective fiction, but as sure as I am sitting in this chair, it is what actually took place. Somewhere from close to, there came the sound of an owl hooting. At the same moment I distinctly heard the noise of what seemed like a scuffle, and a stifled curse. And then—and this is what beats me, sir," McIver pounded a huge fist into an equally huge palm, "I was picked up from behind as if I was a baby. Yes, sir, a baby."

Involuntarily Sir Bryan smiled.

"You make a good substantial infant, McIver."

"Exactly, sir," grunted the Inspector. "If a man had suggested such a thing to me yesterday I'd have laughed in his face. But the fact remains that I was picked up just like a child in arms, and doped, sir, doped. Me—at my time of life. They chloroformed me, and that was the last I saw of Zaboleff or the rest of the gang."

"Yes, but it's the rest of the report that beats me," said his chief thoughtfully.

"So it does me, sir," agreed McIver. "When I came to myself early this morning I didn't realize where I was. Of course my mind at once went back to the preceding night, and what with feeling sick as the result of the chloroform, and sicker at having been fooled, I wasn't too pleased with myself. And then I rubbed my eyes and pinched myself, and for a moment or two I honestly thought I'd gone off my head. There was I sitting on my own front door step, with a cushion all nicely arranged for my head and every single man I'd taken down with me asleep on the pavement outside. I tell you, sir, I looked at those eight fellows all ranged in a row for about five minutes before my brain began to act. I was simply stupefied. And then I began to feel angry. To be knocked on the head by a crew like Flash Jim might happen to anybody. But to be treated like naughty children and sent home to bed was a bit too much. Dammit, I thought, while they were about it, why didn't they tuck me up with my wife."

Once again Sir Bryan smiled, but the other was too engrossed to notice.

"It was then I saw the note," continued McIver. He fumbled in his pocket, and his chief stretched out his hand to see the original. He already knew the contents almost by heart, and the actual note itself threw no additional light on the matter. It was typewritten, and the paper was such as can be bought by the ream at any cheap stationer's.

"To think of an old bird like you, Mac," it ran, "going and showing yourself up in a chink of light. You must tell Mrs. Mac to get some more cushions. There were only enough in the parlour for you and Andrews. I have taken Zaboleff and Waldock, and I dropped Flash Jim in Piccadilly Circus. I flogged two of the others whose method of livelihood failed to appeal to me;

the remaining small fry I turned loose. Cheer oh! old son. The fellow in St. James's makes wonderful pick-me-ups for the morning after. Hope I didn't hurt you."

Idly Sir Bryan studied the note, holding it up to the light to see if there was any watermark on the paper which might help. Then he studied the typed words, and finally with a slight shrug of his shoulders he laid it on the desk in front of him.

"An ordinary Remington, I should think. And as there are several thousands in use it doesn't help much. What about Flash Jim?"

McIver shook his head.

"The first thing I did, sir, was to run him to ground. And I put it across him good and strong. He admitted everything: admitted he was down there, but over the rest of the show he swore by everything that he knew no more than I did. All he could say was that suddenly the room seemed full of men. And the men were all masked. Then he got a clip over the back of the head, and he remembers nothing more till the policeman on duty at Piccadilly Circus woke him with his boot just before dawn this morning."

"Which fact, of course, you have verified," said Sir Bryan.

"At once, sir," answered the other. "For once in his life Flash Jim appears to be speaking the truth. Which puts a funny complexion on matters, sir, if he is speaking the truth."

The Inspector leaned forward and stared at his chief.

"You've heard the rumours, sir," he went on after a moment, "the same as I have."

"Perhaps," said Sir Bryan quietly. "But go on, McIver. I'd like to hear what's on your mind."

"It's the Black Gang, sir," said the Inspector, leaning forward impressively.

"There have been rumours going round, rumours which our men have heard here and there for the past two months. I've heard 'em myself; and once or twice I've wondered. Now I'm sure—especially after what Flash Jim said. That gang is no rumour, it's solid fact."

"Have you any information as to what their activities have been, assuming for a moment it is the truth?" asked Sir Bryan.

"None for certain, sir; until this moment I wasn't certain of its existence. But now—looking back—there have been quite a number of sudden disappearances. We haven't troubled officially, we haven't been asked to. Hardly likely when one realizes who the people are who have disappeared."

"All conjecture, McIver," said Sir Bryan. "They may be lying doggo, or they'll turn up elsewhere."

"They may be, sir," answered McIver doggedly. "But take the complete disappearance of Granger a fortnight ago. He's one of the worst of the Red men, and we know he hasn't left the country. Where is he? His wife, I happen to know, is crazy with anxiety, so it don't look like a put-up job. Take that extraordinary case of the Pole who was found lashed to the railings in Whitehall with one half of his beard and hair shaved off and the motto 'Portrait of a Bolshevist' painted on his forehead. Well, I don't need to tell you, sir, that that particular Pole, Strambowski, was undoubtedly a messenger between—well, we know who between and what the message was. And then take last night."

"Well, what about last night?"

"For the first time this gang has come into direct contact with us."

"Always assuming the fact of its existence."

"Exactly, sir," answered McIver. "Well, they've got Zaboleff and they've got Waldock, and they laid eight of us out to cool. I guess they're not to be sneezed at."

With a thoughtful look on his face Sir Bryan rose and strolled over to the window. Though not prepared to go quite as far as McIver, there were certainly some peculiar elements in the situation—elements which he, as head of a big public department, could not officially allow for an instant, however much it might amuse him as a private individual.

"We must find Zaboleff and Waldock," he said curtly, without turning round. "Waldock, at any rate, has friends who will make a noise unless he's forthcoming. And..."

But his further remarks were interrupted by the entrance of his secretary with a note.

"For the Inspector, Sir Bryan," she said, and McIver after a glance at his chief, opened the envelope. For a while he studied the letter in silence, then with an enigmatic smile he rose and handed it to the man by the window.

"No answer, thank you, Miss Forbes," he said, and when they were once more alone, he began rubbing his hands together softly—a sure sign of being excited. "Curtis and Samuel Bauer, both flogged nearly to death and found in a slum off Whitechapel. The note said two of 'em had been flogged."

"So," said Sir Bryan quietly. "These two were at Barking last night?"

"They were, sir," answered the Inspector.

"And their line?" queried the Chief.

"White slave traffic of the worst type," said McIver. "They generally drug the girls with cocaine or some dope first. What do you say to my theory now, sir?"

"It's another point in its favour, McIver," conceded Sir Bryan cautiously: "but it still wants a lot more proof. And, anyway, whether you're right or not, we can't allow it to continue. We shall be having questions asked in Parliament."

McIver nodded portentously. "If I can't lay my hands on a man who can lift me up like a baby and dope me, may I never have another case. Like a baby, sir. Me——"

He opened his hands out helplessly, and this time Sir Bryan laughed outright, only to turn with a quick frown as the door leading to the secretary's office was flung open to admit a man. He caught a vague glimpse of the scandalized Miss Forbes hovering like a canary eating bird-seed in the background: then he turned to the new-comer.

"Confound it, Hugh," he cried. "I'm busy."

Hugh Drummond grinned all over his face, and lifting a hand like a leg of mutton he smote Sir Bryan in the back, to the outraged amazement of Inspector McIver.

"You priceless old bean," boomed Hugh affably. "I gathered from the female bird punching the what-not outside that the great brain was heaving, but, my dear old lad, I have come to report a crime. A crime which I positively saw committed with my own eyes: an outrage: a blot upon this fair land of ours."

He sank heavily into a chair and selected a cigarette. He was a vast individual with one of those phenomenally ugly faces which is rendered utterly pleasant by the extraordinary charm of its owner's expression. No human being had ever been known to be angry with Hugh for long. He was either moved to laughter by the perennial twinkle in the big man's blue eyes, or he was stunned by a playful blow on the chest from a fist which rivalled a steam hammer. Of brain he apparently possessed a minimum: of muscle he possessed about five ordinary men's share.

And yet unlike so many powerful men his quickness on his feet was astounding—as many a good heavyweight boxer had found to his cost. In the days of his youth Hugh Drummond—known more familiarly to his intimates as Bulldog—had been able to do the hundred in a shade over ten seconds. And though the mere thought of such a performance now would have caused him to break out into a cold sweat, he was still quite capable of a turn of speed which many a lighter-built man would have envied.

Between him and Sir Bryan Johnstone existed one of those friendships which are founded on totally dissimilar tastes. He had been Bryan Johnstone's fag at school, and for some inscrutable reason the quiet scholarship of the elder boy had appealed to the kid of fourteen who was even then a mass of brawn. And when one day Johnstone, going about his lawful occasions as a prefect, discovered young Drummond reducing a boy two years older than himself to a fair semblance of a jelly, the appeal was reciprocated.

"He called you a scut," said Drummond a little breathlessly when his lord and master mildly inquired the reason of the disturbance. "So I scutted him."

It was only too true, and with a faint smile Johnstone watched the "scutted" one depart with undignified rapidity. Then he looked at his fag.

"Thank you, Drummond," he remarked awkwardly.

"Rot. That's all right," returned the other, blushing uncomfortably.

And that was all. But it started then, and it never died, though their ways lay many poles apart. To Johnstone a well-deserved knighthood and a high position in the land: to Drummond as much money as he wanted and a life of sport.

"Has someone stolen the goldfish?" queried Sir Bryan with mild sarcasm.

"Great Scott! I hope not," cried Hugh in alarm. "Phyllis gave me complete instructions about the brutes before she toddled off. I make a noise like an ant's egg, and drop them in the sink every morning, No, old lad of the village, it is something of vast import: a stain upon the escutcheon of your force. Last night—let us whisper it in Gath—I dined and further supped not wisely but too well. In fact I deeply regret to admit that I became a trifle blotto—not to say tanked. Of course it wouldn't have happened if Phyllis had been propping up the jolly old home, don't you know: but she's away in the country with the nightingales and slugs and things. Well, as I say, in the young hours of the morning, I thought I'd totter along home. I'd been with some birds—male birds, Tumkins"—he stared sternly at Sir Bryan, while McIver stiffened into rigid horror at such an incredible nickname—"male birds, playing push halfpenny or some such game of skill or chance. And when I left it was about two a.m. Well, I wandered along through Leicester Square, and stopped just outside Scott's to let one of those watering carts water my head for me. Deuced considerate driver he was too: stopped his horse for a couple of minutes and let one jet play on me uninterruptedly. Well, as I say, while I was lying in the road, steaming at the brow, a motor car went past, and it stopped in Piccadilly Circus."

McIver's air of irritation vanished suddenly, and a quick glance passed between him and Sir Bryan.

"Nothing much you observe in that, Tumkins," he burbled on, quite unconscious of the sudden attention of his hearers. "But wait, old lad—I haven't got to the motto yet. From this car there stepped large numbers of men: at least, so it seemed to me, and you must remember I'd recently had a shampoo. And just as I got abreast of them they lifted out another warrior, who appeared to me to be unconscious. At first I thought there were two, until I focussed the old optics and found I'd been squinting. They put him on the pavement and got back into the car again just as I tottered alongside.

"'What ho! souls,' I murmured, 'what is this and that, so to speak?'

"'Binged, old bean, badly binged,' said the driver of the car. 'We're leaving him there to cool.'

"And with that the car drove off. There was I, Tumkins, in a partially binged condition alone in Piccadilly Circus with a bird in a completely binged condition.

"'How now,' I said to myself. 'Shall I go and induce yon water merchant to return'—as a matter of fact I was beginning to feel I could do with another whack myself—'or shall I leave you here—as your pals observed—to cool?'

"I bent over him as I pondered this knotty point, and as I did so, Tumkins, I became aware of a strange smell."

Hugh paused dramatically and selected another cigarette, while Sir Bryan flashed a quick glance of warning at McIver, who was obviously bursting with suppressed excitement.

"A peculiar and sickly odour, Tumkins," resumed the speaker with maddening deliberation. "A strange and elusive perfume. For a long time it eluded me—that smell: I just couldn't place it. And then suddenly I got it: right in the middle, old boy—plumb in the centre of the windpipe. It was chloroform: the bird wasn't drunk—he was doped."

Completely exhausted Hugh lay back in his chair, and once again Sir Bryan flashed a warning glance at his exasperated subordinate.

"Would you be able to recognize any of the men in the car if you saw them again?" he asked quietly.

"I should know the driver," answered Hugh after profound thought. "And the bird beside him. But not the others."

"Did you take the number of the car?" snapped McIver.

"My dear old man," murmured Hugh in a pained voice, "who on earth ever does take the number of a car? Except your warriors, who always get it wrong. Besides, as I tell you, I was partially up the pole."

"What did you do then?" asked Sir Bryan.

"Well, I brought the brain to bear," answered Hugh, "and decided there was nothing to do. He was doped, and I was bottled—so by a unanimous casting vote of one—I toddled off home. But Tumkins, while I was feeding the goldfish this morning—or rather after lunch—conscience was gnawing at my vitals. And after profound meditation, and consulting with my fellow Denny, I decided that the call of duty was clear. I came to you, Tumkins, as a child flies to its mother. Who better, I thought, than old Tum-tum to listen to my maidenly secrets? And so..."

"One moment, Hugh," Sir Bryan held up his hand. "Do you mind if I speak to Inspector McIver for a moment?"

"Anything you like, old lad," murmured Drummond. "But be merciful. Remember my innocent wife in the country."

And silence settled on the room, broken only by the low-voiced conversation between McIver and his chief in the window. By their gestures it seemed as if Sir Bryan was suggesting something to his subordinate to which that worthy officer was a little loath to agree. And after a while a strangled snore from the chair announced that Drummond was ceasing to take an intelligent interest in things mundane.

"He's an extraordinary fellow, McIver," said Sir Bryan, glancing at the sleeper with a smile. "I've known him ever since we were boys at school. And he's not quite such a fool as he makes himself out. You remember that extraordinary case over the man Peterson a year or so ago. Well, it was he who did the whole thing. His complete disability to be cunning utterly defeated that master-crook, who was always looking for subtlety that wasn't there. And of course his strength is absolutely phenomenal."

"I know, sir," said McIver doubtfully, "but would he consent to take on such a job—and do exactly as he was told?"

They were both looking out of the window, while in the room behind them the heavy breathing of the sleeper rose and fell monotonously. And when the whole audience is asleep it ceases to be necessary to talk in undertones. Which was why Sir Bryan and the Inspector during the next ten minutes discussed certain matters of import which they would not have discussed through megaphones at the Savoy. They concerned Hugh and other things, and the other things particularly were of interest. And they continued discussing these other things until, with a dreadful noise like a racing motor back-firing, the sleeper sat up in his chair and stretched himself.

"Tumkins," he cried. "I have committed sacrilege. I have slept in the Holy of Holies. Have you decided on my fate? Am I to be shot at dawn?"

Sir Bryan left the window and sat down at his desk. For a moment or two he rubbed his chin thoughtfully with his left hand, as if trying to make up his mind: then he lay back in his chair and stared at his erstwhile fag.

"Would you like to do a job of work, old man?"

Hugh started as if he had been stung by a wasp, and Sir Bryan smiled.

"Not real work," he said reassuringly. "But by mere luck last night you saw something which Inspector McIver would have given a good deal to see. Or to be more accurate, you saw some men whom McIver particularly wants to meet."

"Those blokes in the car, you mean," cried Hugh brightly.

"Those blokes in the car," agreed the other. "Incidentally, I may say there was a good deal more in that little episode than you think: and after consultation with McIver I have decided to tell you a certain amount about it, because you can help us, Hugh. You see, you're one up on McIver: you have at any rate seen those men and he hasn't. Moreover, you say you could recognize two of them again."

"Good heavens! Tumkins," murmured Hugh aghast, "don't say you want me to tramp the streets of London looking for them."

Sir Bryan smiled.

"We'll spare you that," he answered. "But I'd like you to pay attention to what I'm going to tell you."

Hugh's face assumed the look of intense pain always indicative of thought in its owner.

"Carry on, old bird," he remarked. "I'll try and last the course."

"Last night," began Sir Bryan quietly, "a very peculiar thing happened to McIver. I won't worry you with the full details, and it will be enough if I just give you a bare outline of what occurred. He and some of his men in the normal course of duty surrounded a certain house in which were some people we wanted to lay our hands on. To be more accurate there was one man there whom we wanted. He'd been shadowed ever since he'd landed in England that morning, shadowed the whole way from the docks to the house. And sure enough when McIver and his men surrounded the house, there was our friend and all his pals in one of the downstairs rooms. It was then that this peculiar thing happened. I gather from McIver that he heard the noise of an owl hooting, also a faint scuffle and a curse. And after that he heard nothing more. He was chloroformed from behind, and went straight out of the picture."

"Great Scott!" murmured Hugh, staring incredulously at McIver. "What an amazing thing!"

"And this is where you come in, Hugh," continued Sir Bryan.

"Me!" Hugh sat up abruptly. "Why me?"

"One of the men inside the room was an interesting fellow known as Flash Jim. He is a burglar of no mean repute, though he is quite ready to tackle any sort of job which carries money with it. And when McIver, having recovered himself this morning, ran Flash Jim to ground in one of his haunts, he was quite under the impression that the men who had doped him and the other officers were pals of Flash Jim. But after he'd talked to him he changed his mind. All Flash Jim could tell him was that on the previous night he and some friends had been discussing business at this house. He didn't attempt to deny that. He went on to say that suddenly the room had been filled with a number of masked men, and that he'd had a clip over the back of the head which knocked him out. After that presumably he was given a whiff of chloroform to keep him quiet, and the next thing he remembers is being kicked into activity by the policeman at—" Sir Bryan paused a moment to emphasize the point—"at Piccadilly Circus."

"Good Lord!" said Hugh dazedly. "Then that bird I saw last night sleeping it off on the pavement was Flash Jim."

"Precisely," answered Sir Bryan. "But what is far more to the point, old man, is that the two birds you think you would be able to recognize and who were in the car, are two of the masked men who first of all laid out McIver and subsequently surrounded Flash Jim and his pals inside."

"But what did they want to do that for?" asked Hugh in bewilderment.

"That is just what we want to find out," replied Sir Bryan. "As far as we can see at the moment they are not criminals in the accepted sense of the word. They flogged two of the men who were there last night, and there are no two men in England who more richly deserved it. They kidnapped two others, one of whom was the man we particularly wanted. Then to wind up, they planted Flash Jim as I've told you, let the others go, and brought McIver and all his men back to McIver's house, where they left them to cool on the pavement."

For a moment there was silence, and then Hugh began to shake with laughter.

"But how perfectly priceless!" he spluttered when he was able to speak once more. "Old Algy will burst a blood-vessel when I tell him: you know, Algy, Tumkins, don't you—that bird with the eyeglass, and the funny-looking face?"

Inspector McIver frowned heavily. All along he had doubted the wisdom of telling Drummond anything: now he felt that his misgivings were confirmed. What on earth was the good of expecting such an obvious ass to be of the smallest assistance? And now this raucous hilarity struck him as being positively indecent. But the Chief had insisted: the responsibility was his. One thing was certain, reflected McIver grimly. Algy, whoever he was, would not be the only one to whom the privilege of bursting a blood-vessel would be accorded. And before very long it would be all round London—probably in the papers. And McIver particularly did not want that to happen. However, the next instant Sir Bryan soothed some of his worst fears.

"Under no circumstances, Hugh," he remarked gravely, "is Algy to be given a chance of bursting any blood-vessel. You understand what I mean. What I have said to you this afternoon is for you alone—and no one else. We know it: Flash Jim and Co. know it."

"And the jolly old masked sportsmen know it," said Hugh.

"Quite," remarked Sir Bryan. "And that's a deuced sight too many already. We don't want any more."

"As far as I am concerned, my brave Tumkins," cried the other, "the list is closed. Positively not another participator in the stable secret. But I still don't see where I leap in and join the fray."

"This way, old boy," said Sir Bryan. "McIver is a very strong man, and yet he was picked up last night as he himself says as if he was a baby, by one of these masked men who, judging from a note he wrote, is presumably the leader of the gang. And so we deduce that this leader is something exceptional in the way of strength."

"By Gad! that's quick, Tumkins," said Hugh admiringly. "But then you always did have the devil of a brain."

"Now you are something very exceptional in that line, Hugh," continued the other.

"Oh! I can push a fellah's face if it's got spots and things," said Hugh deprecatingly.

"And what I want to know is this. If we give you warning would you care to go with McIver the next time he has any job on, where he thinks it is likely this gang may turn up? We have a pretty shrewd idea as to the type of thing they specialize in."

Hugh passed his hand dazedly over his forehead.

"Sort of mother's help you mean," and McIver frowned horribly. "While the bird biffs McIver, I biff the bird. Is that the notion?"

"That is the notion," agreed Sir Bryan. "Of course you'll have to do exactly what McIver tells you, and the whole thing is most unusual. But in view of the special features of the case.... What is it, Miss Forbes?" He glanced up at his secretary, who was standing in the doorway, with a slight frown.

"He insists on seeing you at once, Sir Bryan."

She came forward with a card, which Sir Bryan took.

"Charles Latter." The frown deepened. "What the deuce does he want?"

The answer was supplied by the gentleman himself, who appeared at that moment in the doorway. He was evidently in a state of great agitation and Sir Bryan rose.

"I am engaged at the moment, Mr. Latter," he said coldly.

"My business won't take you a minute, Sir Bryan," he cried. "But what I want to know is this. Is this country civilized or is it not? Look at what I received by the afternoon post."

He handed a sheet of paper to the other, who glanced at it casually. Then suddenly the casual look vanished, and Sir Bryan sat down at his desk, his eyes grim and stern.

"By the afternoon post, you say."

"Yes. And there have been too many disappearances lately!"

"How did you know that?" snapped the chief, staring at him.

For a moment Latter hesitated and changed colour.

"Oh! everyone knows it," he answered, trying to speak casually.

"Everyone does not know it," remarked Sir Bryan quietly. "However, you did quite right to come to me. What are your plans during the next few days?"

"I am going out of London to-morrow to stay with Lady Manton near Sheffield," answered Latter. "A semi-political house party. Good heavens! What's that?"

With a snort Hugh sat up blinking.

"So sorry, old lad," he burbled. "I snored: know I did. Late hours are the devil, aren't they?"

He heaved himself out of his chair, and grinned pleasantly at Latter, who frowned disapprovingly.

"I don't go in for them myself. Well, Sir Bryan."

"This matter shall be attended to, Mr. Latter. I will see to it. Good afternoon. I will keep this note."

"And who was that little funny-face?" said Hugh as the door closed behind Mr. Latter.

"Member of Parliament for a north country constituency," answered Sir Bryan, still staring at the piece of paper in his hand. "Lives above his income. Keenly ambitious. But I thought he was all right."

The other two stared at him in surprise.

"What do you mean, sir?" asked McIver at length.

"Our unknown friends do not think so, Mac," answered the chief, handing his subordinate the note left by Latter. "They are beginning to interest me, these gentlemen."

"You need a rest, Charles Latter," read McIver slowly. "We have established a home for people like you where several of your friends await you. In a few days you will join them."

"There are two things which strike one, McIver," remarked Sir Bryan, thoughtfully lighting a cigarette. "First and most important: that message and the one you found this morning were written on the same typewriter—the letter 'e' is distorted in each case. And, secondly, Mr. Charles Latter appears to have inside information concerning the recent activities of our masked friends which it is difficult to see how he came by. Unless"—he paused and stared out of the window with a frown—"unless they are far more conversant with his visiting list than I am."

McIver's great jaw stuck out as if made of granite.

"It proves my theory, sir," he grunted, "but if those jokers try that game on with Mr. Latter they won't catch me a second time."

A terrific blow on the back made him gasp and splutter.

"There speaks my hero-boy," cried Hugh. "Together we will outwit the knaves. I will write and cancel a visit: glad of the chance. Old Julia Manton—face like a horse: house at Sheffield: roped me in, Tumkins—positively stunned me with her verbosity. Ghastly house—but reeks of boodle."

Sir Bryan looked at him surprised.

"Do you mean to say you are going to Lady Manton's?"

"I was. But not now. I will stick closer than a brother to Mr. McIver."

"I think not, old man. You go. If you'd been awake you'd have heard Latter say that he was going there too. You can be of use sooner than I thought."

"Latter going to old Julia?" Hugh stared at him amazed. "My dear old Tum-tum, what a perfectly amazing coincidence."

3

In which Hugh Drummond
composes a letter

Hugh Drummond strolled slowly along Whitehall in the direction of Trafalgar Square. His face wore its habitual look of vacuous good humour, and at intervals he hummed a little tune under his breath. It was outside the Carlton that he paused as a car drew up by his side, and a man and a girl got out.

"Algy, my dear old boy," he murmured, taking off his hat, "are we in health to-day?"

"Passable, old son," returned Algy Longworth, adjusting his quite unnecessary eyeglass. "The oysters wilted a bit this morning, but I'm trying again to-night. By the way, do you know Miss Farreydale?"

Hugh bowed.

"You know the risk you run, I suppose, going with about him?"

The girl laughed. "He seems harmless," she answered lightly.

"That's his guile. After the second cup of tea he's a perfect devil. By the same token, Algy, I am hibernating awhile in the country. Going to dear old Julia Manton's for a few days. Up Sheffield way."

Miss Farreydale looked at him with a puzzled frown.

"Do you mean Lady Manton—Sir John's wife?"

"That's the old dear," returned Hugh. "Know her?"

"Fairly well. But her name isn't Julia. And she won't love you if you call her old."

"Good heavens! Isn't it? And won't she? I must be mixing her up with someone else."

"Dorothy Manton is a well-preserved woman of—shall we say—thirty-five? She was a grocer's daughter: she is now a snob of the worst type. I hope you'll enjoy yourself."

"Your affection for her stuns me," murmured Hugh. "I appear to be in for a cheerful time."

"When do you go, Hugh?" asked Algy.

"To-morrow, old man. But I'm keeping you from your tea. Keep the table between you after the second cup, Miss Farreydale."

He lifted his hat and walked on up the Haymarket, only to turn back suddenly.

"'Daisy,' you said, didn't you?"

"No. Dorothy," laughed the girl. "Come on, Algy, I want my tea."

She passed into the Carlton, and for a moment the two men were together on the pavement.

"Lucky she knows the Manton woman," murmured Hugh.

"Don't you?" gasped Algy.

"Not from Eve, old son. Don't fix up anything in the near future. We shall be busy. I've joined the police and shall require help."

With a cheery nod he strolled off, and after a moment's hesitation Algy Longworth followed the girl into the Carlton.

"Mad, isn't he—your friend?" she remarked as he came up.

"Absolutely," he answered. "Let's masticate an éclair."!

A quarter of an hour later Hugh let himself into his house in Brook Street. On the hall table were three telegrams which he opened and read. Then, having torn them into tiny fragments, he went on into his study and rang the bell.

"Beer, Denny," he remarked, as his servant came in. "Beer in a mug. I am prostrate. And then bring me one of those confounded books which people have their names put in followed by the usual lies."

"'Who's Who,' sir," said Denny,

"You've got it," said his master. "Though who is who these days, Denny, is a very dark matter. I am rapidly losing my faith in my brother man—rapidly. And then after that we have to write a letter to Julia—no, Dorothy Manton—erstwhile grocer's daughter, with whom I propose to dally for a few days."

"I don't seem to know the name, sir."

"Nor did I, Denny, until about an hour ago. But I have it on reliable authority that she exists."

"But how, sir..." began the bewildered Denny.

24

"At the moment the way is dark," admitted Drummond. "The fog of war enwraps me. Beer, fool, beer."

Accustomed to the little vagaries of his master, Denny left the room to return shortly with a large jug of beer which he placed on a small table beside Drummond's chair. Then he waited motionless behind his chair with a pencil and writing-block in his hand.

"A snob, Denny; a snob," said Drummond at length, putting down his empty glass. "How does one best penetrate into the life and home of a female snob whom one does not even know by sight? Let us reason from first principles. What have we in our repertoire that would fling wide the portals of her house, revealing to our awestruck gaze all the footmen ranged in a row?" He rose suddenly. "I've got it, Denny; at least some of it. We have old Turniptop. Is he not a cousin of mine?"

"You mean Lord Staveley, sir," said Denny diffidently.

"Of course I do, you ass. Who else?" Clasping his replenished glass of beer, Hugh strode up and down the room. "Somehow or other we must drag him in."

"He's in Central Africa, sir," reminded Denny cautiously.

"What the devil does that matter? Julia—I mean Dorothy—won't know. Probably never heard of the poor old thing. Write, fool; take your pen and write quickly."

"'Dear Lady Manton,

"'I hope you have not forgotten the pleasant few days we spent together at Wiltshire Towers this spring.'"

"But you didn't go to the Duke's this spring, sir," gasped Denny.

"I know that, you ass—but no more did she. To be exact, the place was being done up, only she won't know. Go on, I'm going to overflow again."

"'I certainly have not forgotten the kind invitation you gave to my cousin Staveley and myself to come and stop with you. He, at the moment, is killing beasts in Africa: whereas I am condemned to this unpleasant country. To-morrow I have to go to Sheffield, ...'"

He paused. "Why, Denny—why do I have to go to Sheffield? Why in heaven's name does any one ever go to Sheffield?"

"They make knives there, sir."

"Do they? But you needn't go there to buy them. And anyway, I don't want knives."

"You might just say on business, sir," remarked his servant.

"Gad! you're a genius, Denny. Put that in. 'Sheffield on business, and I wondered if I might take you at your word and come to...' Where's the bally woman live? Look it up in 'Who's Who.'"

"Drayton House, sir," announced Denny.

"'To Drayton House for a day or two. Yours very sincerely.'

"That'll do the trick, Denny. Give it to me, and I'll write it out."

"A piece of the best paper with the crest and telephone number embossed in blue, and the victory is ours."

"Aren't you giving her rather short notice, sir," said Denny doubtfully.

Drummond laid down his pen and stared at him sadly.

"Sometimes, Denny, I despair of you," he answered. "Even after four years of communion with me there are moments when you relapse into your pristine brain wallow. If I gave her any longer it is just conceivable—though, I admit, not likely—that I might get my answer from her stating that she was completely unaware of my existence, and that she'd sent my letter to the police. And where should we be then, my faithful varlet? As it is, I shall arrive at Drayton House just after the letter, discover with horror that I have made a mistake, and be gracefully forgiven by my charming hostess as befits a man with such exalted friends. Now run away and get me a taxi."

"Will you be in to dinner, sir?"

"Perhaps—perhaps not. In case I'm not, I shall go up to Sheffield in the Rolls to-morrow. See that everything is packed."

"Will you want me to come with you, sir?"

"No, Denny—not this time. I have a sort of premonition that I'm going to enjoy myself at Drayton House, and you're too young for that sort of thing."

With a resigned look on his face, Denny left the room, closing the door gently behind him. But Drummond, left to himself, did not at once continue his letter to Lady Manton. With his pen held loosely in his hand he sat at his desk staring thoughtfully at the wall opposite. Gone completely was his customary inane look of good humour: in its place was an expression of quiet, almost grim, determination. He had the air of a man faced with big decisions, and to whom, moreover, such an experience was no novelty. For some five minutes he sat there motionless; then with a short laugh he came out of his reverie.

"We're getting near the motto, my son," he muttered—"deuced near. If we don't draw the badger in a few weeks, I'll eat my hat."

With another laugh he turned once more to his half-finished letter. And a minute or two later, having stamped and addressed the envelope, he slipped it into his pocket and rose. He crossed the room and unlocked a small safe which stood in the corner. From it he took a small automatic revolver which he dropped into his coat pocket, also a tiny bundle of what looked like fine black silk. Then, having relocked the safe he picked up his hat and stick and went into the hall.

"Denny," he called, pausing by the front door.

"Sir," answered that worthy, appearing from the back premises.

"If Mr. Darrell or any of them ring up I shall be tearing a devilled bone to-night at the Savoy grill at eleven o'clock."

4

In which Count Zadowa
gets a shock

Number 5, Green Street, Hoxton, was not a prepossessing abode. A notice on one of the dingy downstair windows announced that Mr. William Atkinson was prepared to advance money on suitable security: a visit during business hours revealed that this was no more than the truth, even if the appearance of Mr. Atkinson's minion caused the prospective borrower to wonder how he had acquired such an aggressively English name.

The second and third floors were apparently occupied by his staff, which seemed unduly large considering the locality and quality of his business. Hoxton is hardly in that part of London where large sums of money might be expected to change hands, and yet there was no doubt that Mr. William Atkinson's staff was both large and busy. So busy indeed were his clerks that frequently ten and eleven o'clock at night found them still working hard, though the actual business of the day downstairs concluded at six o'clock—eight Saturdays.

It was just before closing time on the day after the strange affair down at Barking that a large, unkempt-looking individual presented himself at Mr. Atkinson's office. His most pressing need would have seemed to the casual observer to be soap and water, but his appearance apparently excited no surprise in the assistant downstairs. Possibly Hoxton is tolerant of such trifles.

The clerk—a pale, anæmic-looking man with an unhealthy skin and a hook nose—rose wearily from his rest.

"What do you want?" he demanded morosely.

"Wot d'yer think!" retorted the other. "Cat's meat?"

The clerk recoiled, and the blood mounted angrily to his sallow face.

"Don't you use that tone with me, my man," he said angrily. "I'd have you to know that this is my office."

"Yus," answered the other. "Same as it's your nose sitting there like a lump o' putty stuck on to a suet pudding. And if I 'ave any o' your lip, I'll pull it off—see. Throw it outside, I will, and you after it—you parboiled lump of bad tripe. Nah then—business." With a blow that shook the office he thumped the desk with a huge fist. "I ain't got no time to waste—even if you 'ave. 'Ow much?"

He threw a pair of thick hob-nailed boots on to the counter, and stood glaring at the other.

"Two bob," said the clerk indifferently, throwing down a coin and picking up the boots.

"Two bob!" cried the other wrathfully. "Two bob, you miserable Sheenie." For a moment or two he spluttered inarticulately as if speech was beyond him; then his huge hand shot out and gripped the clerk by the collar. "Think again, Archibald," he continued quietly, "think again and think better."

But the assistant, as might be expected in one of his calling, was prepared for emergencies of this sort. Very gently his right hand slid along the counter towards a concealed electric bell which communicated with the staff upstairs. It fulfilled several purposes, that bell: it acted as a call for help or as a warning, and according to the number of times it was pressed, the urgency of the matter could be interpreted by those who heard it. Just now the clerk decided that two rings would meet the case: he disliked the appearance of the large and angry man in whose grip he felt absolutely powerless, and he felt he would like help—very urgently. And so it was perhaps a little unfortunate for him that he should have allowed an ugly little smirk to adorn his lips a second or two before his hand found the bell. The man facing him across the counter saw that smirk and lost his temper in earnest. With a grunt of rage he hit the other square between the eyes, and the clerk collapsed in a huddled heap behind the counter with the bell still unrung.

For a few moments the big man stood motionless, listening intently. From upstairs came the faint tapping of a typewriter; from outside the usual street noises of London came softly through the two closed doors. Then, with an agility remarkable in one so big, he vaulted the counter and inspected the recumbent assistant with a professional eye. A faint grin spread over his face as he noted that gentleman's condition, but after that he wasted no time. So quickly and methodically in fact did he set about things, that it seemed as if the whole performance must have been cut and dried beforehand, even to the temporary disposition of the clerk. In half a minute he was bound and gagged and deposited under the counter. Beside him the big man placed the pair of boots, attached to which was a piece of paper which he took from his pocket. On it was scrawled in an illiterate hand:

"Have took a fare price for the boots, yer swine." Then quite deliberately the big man forced the till and removed some money, after which he once more examined the unconscious man under the counter.

"Without a hitch," he muttered. "Absolutely according to Cocker. Now, old lad of the village, we come to the second item on the programme. That must be the door I want."

He opened it cautiously, and the subdued hum of voices from above came a little louder, to his ears. Then like a shadow he vanished into the semi-darkness of the house upstairs.

*****

It was undoubtedly a house of surprises, was Number 5, Green Street. A stranger passing through the dingy office on the ground floor where Mr. Atkinson's assistant was wont to sit at the receipt of custom, and then ascending the stairs to the first storey would have found it hard to believe that he was in the same house. But then, strangers were not encouraged to do anything of the sort.

There was a door at the top of the flight of stairs, and it was at this door that the metamorphosis took place. On one side of it the stairs ran carpetless and none too clean to the ground floor, on the other side the picture changed. A wide passage with rooms leading out of it from either side confronted the explorer—a passage which was efficiently illuminated with electric lights hung from the ceiling, and the floor of which was covered with a good plain carpet. Along the walls ran rows of book-shelves stretching, save for the gaps at the doors, as far as a partition which closed the further end of the passage. In this partition was another door, and beyond this second door the passage continued to a window tightly shuttered and bolted. From this continuation only one room led off—a room which would have made the explorer rub his eyes in surprise. It was richly—almost luxuriously furnished. In the centre stood a big roll-top writing desk, while scattered about were several arm-chairs upholstered in green leather. A long table almost filled one side of the room; a table covered with every imaginable newspaper. A huge safe flush with the wall occupied the other side, while the window, like the one outside, was almost hermetically sealed. There was a fireplace in the corner, but there was no sign of any fire having been lit, or of any preparations for lighting one. Two electric heaters attached by long lengths of flex to plugs in the wall comprised the heating arrangements, while a big central light and half-a-dozen movable ones illuminated every corner of the room.

In blissful ignorance of the sad plight of the clerk below, two men were sitting in this room, deep in conversation. In a chair drawn up close to the desk was no less a person than Charles Latter, M.P., and it was he who was doing most of the talking. But it was the other man who riveted attention: the man who presumably was Mr. Atkinson himself. He was seated in a swivel chair which he had slewed round so as to face the speaker, and it was his appearance which caught the eye and then held it fascinated.

At first he seemed to be afflicted with an almost phenomenal stoop, and it was only when one got nearer that the reason was clear. The man was a hunchback, and the effect it gave was that of a huge bird of prey. Unlike most hunchbacks, his legs were of normal length, and as he sat motionless in his chair, a hand on each knee, staring with unwinking eyes at his talkative companion, there was something menacing and implacable in his appearance. His hair was grey; his features stern and hard; while his mouth reminded one of a steel trap. But it was his eyes that dominated everything—grey-blue and piercing, they seemed able to probe one's innermost soul. A man to whom it would be unwise to lie—a man utterly unscrupulous in himself, who would yet punish double dealing in those who worked for him with merciless severity. A dangerous man.

"So you went to the police, Mr. Latter," he remarked suavely. "And what had our friend Sir Bryan Johnstone to say on the matter?"

"At first, Count, he didn't say much. In fact he really said very little all through. But once he looked at the note his whole manner changed. I could see that instantly. There was something about the note which interested him...."

"Let me see it," said the Count, holding out his hand.

"I left it with Sir Bryan," answered the other. "He asked me to let him keep it. And he promised that I should be all right."

The Count's lips curled.

"It would take more than Sir Bryan Johnstone's promise, Mr. Latter, to ensure your safety. Do you know whom that note was from?"

"I thought, Count," said the other a little tremulously—"I thought it might be from this mysterious Black Gang that one has heard rumours about."

"It was," replied the Count tersely.

"Heavens!" stammered Latter. "Then it's true; they exist."

"In the last month," answered the hunchback, staring fixedly at his frightened companion, "nearly twenty of our most useful men have disappeared. They have simply vanished into thin air. I know, no matter how, that it is not the police: the police are as mystified as we are. But the police, Mr. Latter, whatever views they may take officially, are in all probability unofficially very glad of our friends' disappearance. At any rate until last night."

"What do you mean?" asked the other.

"Last night the police were baulked of their prey, and McIver doesn't like being baulked. You know Zaboleff was sent over?"

"Yes, of course. That is one of the reasons I came round to-night. Have you seen him?"

"I have not," answered the Count grimly. "The police found out he was coming."

Mr. Latter's face blanched: the thought of Zaboleff in custody didn't appeal to him. It may be mentioned that his feelings were purely selfish—Zaboleff knew too much.

But the Count was speaking again. A faint sneer was on his face; he had read the other's mind like an open book.

"And so," he continued, "did the Black Gang. They removed Zaboleff and our friend Waldock from under the very noses of the police, and, like the twenty others, they have disappeared.

"My God!" There was no doubt now about Mr. Latter's state of mind. "And now they've threatened me."

"And now they've threatened you," agreed the Count. "And you, I am glad to say, have done exactly what I should have told you to do, had I seen you sooner. You have gone to the police."

"But—but," stammered Latter, "the police were no good to Zaboleff last night."

"And it is quite possible," returned the other calmly, "that they will be equally futile in your case. Candidly, Mr. Latter, I am completely indifferent on the subject of your future. You have served our purpose, and all that matters is that you happen to be the bone over which the dogs are going to fight. Until last night the dogs hadn't met—officially; and in the rencontre last night, the police dog, unless I'm greatly mistaken, was caught by surprise. McIver doesn't let that happen twice. In your case he'll be ready. With luck this cursed Black

Gang, who are infinitely more nuisance to me than the police have been or ever will be, will get bitten badly."

Mr. Latter was breathing heavily.

"But what do you want me to do, Count?"

"Nothing at all, except what you were going to do normally," answered the other. He glanced at a notebook on his desk. "You were going to Lady Manton's near Sheffield, I see. Don't alter your plans—go. In all probability it will take place at her house." He glanced contemptuously at the other's somewhat green face, and his manner changed abruptly. "You understand, Mr. Latter," his voice was deadly smooth and quiet, "you understand, don't you, what I say? You will go to Lady Manton's house as arranged, and you will carry on exactly as if you had never received this note. Because, if you don't, if you attempt any tricks with me, whatever the Black Gang may do or may not do to you—however much the police may protect you or may not protect you—you will have us to reckon with. And you know what that means."

"Supposing the gang gets me and foils the police," muttered Latter through dry lips. "What then?"

"I shall deal with them personally. They annoy me."

There was something so supremely confident in the tone of the Count's voice, that the other man looked at him quickly.

"But have you any idea who they are?" he asked eagerly.

"None—at present. Their leader is clever—but so am I. They have deliberately elected to fight me, and now I have had enough. It will save trouble if the police catch them for me: but if not..."

The Count shrugged his shoulders, and with a gesture of his hand dismissed the matter. Then he picked up a piece of paper from the desk and glanced at it.

"I will now give you your orders for Sheffield," he continued. "It has been reported to me that in Sir John Manton's works there is a red-hot madman named Delmorlick. He has a good job himself, but he spends most of his spare time inciting the unemployed—of which I am glad to say there are large numbers in the town—to absurd deeds of violence. He is a very valuable man to us, and appears to be one of those extraordinary beings who really believe in the doctrines of Communism. He can lash a mob, they tell me, into an absolute frenzy with his tongue. I want you to seek him out, and give him fifty pounds to carry on with. Tell him, of course, that it comes from the Great Master in Russia, and spur him on to renewed activity.

"You will also employ him, and two or three others whom you must leave him to choose, to carry out a little scheme of which you will find full details in this letter." He handed an envelope to Latter, who took it with a trembling hand. "You personally will make arrangements about the necessary explosives. I calculate that, if successful, it should throw at least three thousand more men out of work. Moreover, Mr. Latter, if it is successful your fee will be a thousand pounds."

"A thousand!" muttered Latter. "Is there much danger?"

The count smiled contemptuously. "Not if you do your work properly. Hullo! What's up?"

From a little electric bell at his elbow came four shrill rings, repeated again and again.

The count rose, and with systematic thoroughness swept every piece of paper off the desk into his pocket. Then he shut down the top and locked it, while the bell, a little muffled, still rang inside.

"What's the fool doing?" he cried angrily, stepping over to the big safe let into the wall, while Latter, his face white and terrified, followed at his side. And then abruptly the bell stopped.

Very deliberately the count pressed two concealed knobs, so sunk into the wall as to be invisible to a stranger, and the door of the safe swung open. And only then was it obvious that the safe was not a safe, but a second exit leading to a flight of stairs. For a moment or two he stood motionless, listening intently, while Latter fidgeted at his side. One hand was on a master switch which controlled all the lights, the other on a knob inside the second passage which, when turned, would close the great steel door noiselessly behind them.

He was frowning angrily, but gradually the frown was replaced by a look of puzzled surprise. Four rings from the shop below was the recognized signal for urgent danger, and everybody's plan of action was cut and dried for such an emergency. In the other rooms every book and paper in the slightest degree incriminating were hurled pell-mell into secret recesses in the floor which had been specially constructed under every table. In their place appeared books carefully and very skilfully faked, purporting to record the business transactions of Mr. William Atkinson. And in the event of surprise being expressed at the size of Mr. Atkinson's business considering the sort of office he possessed below, and the type of his clientele, it would soon be seen that Hoxton was but one of several irons which that versatile gentleman had in the fire. There were indisputable proofs in indisputable ledgers that Mr. Atkinson had organized similar enterprises in several of the big towns of England and Scotland, to say nothing of a large West End branch run under the name of Lewer Brothers. And surely he had the perfect right, if he so wished, to establish his central office in Hoxton ... Or Timbuctoo ... What the devil did it matter to anyone except himself?

In the big room at the end the procedure was even simpler. The Count merely passed through the safe door and vanished through his private bolt-hole, leaving everything in darkness. And should inconvenient visitors ask inconvenient questions—well, it was Mr. Atkinson's private office, and a very nice office too, though at the moment he was away.

Thus the procedure—simple and sound; but on this occasion something seemed to have gone wrong. Instead of the industrious silence of clerks working overtime on affairs of financial import in Edinburgh and Manchester, a perfect babel of voices became audible in the passage. And then there came an agitated knocking on the door.

"Who is it?" cried the Count sharply. It may be mentioned that even the most influential members of his staff knew better than to come into the room without previously obtaining permission.

"It's me, sir—Cohen," came an agitated voice from outside.

For a moment the Count paused: then with a turn of the knob he closed the safe door silently. With an imperious hand he waved Latter to a chair, and resumed his former position at the desk.

"Come in," he snapped.

It was a strange and unwholesome object that obeyed the order, and the Count sat back in his chair.

"What the devil have you been doing?"

A pair of rich blue-black eyes, and a nose from which traces of blood still trickled had not improved the general appearance of the assistant downstairs. In one hand he carried a pair of hobnail boots, in the other a piece of paper, and he brandished them alternately while a flood of incoherent frenzy burst from his lips.

For a minute or two the Count listened, until his first look of surprise gave way to one of black anger.

"Am I to understand, you wretched little worm," he snarled, "that you gave the urgency danger signal, not once but half a dozen times merely because a man hit you over the nose?"

"But he knocked me silly, sir," quavered the other. "And when I came to, and saw the boots lying beside me and the till opened, I kind of lost my head. I didn't know what had happened, sir—and I thought I'd better ring the bell—in case of trouble."

He retreated a step or two towards the door, terrified out of his wits by the look of diabolical fury in the hunchback's eyes. Three or four clerks, who had been surreptitiously peeping through the open door, melted rapidly away, while from his chair Mr. Latter watched the scene fascinated. He was reminded of a bird and a snake, and suddenly he gave a little shudder as he realized that his own position was in reality much the same as that of the unfortunate Cohen.

And then just as the tension was becoming unbearable there came the interruption. Outside in the passage, clear and distinct, there sounded twice the hoot of an owl. To Mr. Latter it meant nothing; to the frightened little Jew it meant nothing; but on the Count the effect was electrical. With a quickness incredible in one so deformed he was at the door, and into the passage, hurling Cohen out of his way into a corner. His powerful fists were clenched by his side: the veins in his neck were standing out like whipcord. But to Mr. Latter's surprise he made no movement, and rising from his chair he too peered round the door along the passage, only to stagger back after a second or two with a feeling of sick fear in his soul, and a sudden dryness in the throat. For twenty yards away, framed in the doorway at the head of the stairs leading down to the office below, he had seen a huge, motionless figure. For a perceptible time he had stared at it, and it had seemed to stare at him. Then the door had shut, and on the other side a key had turned. And the figure had been draped from head to foot in black....

5

In which Charles Latter, M.P., goes mad

Drummond arrived at Drayton House just as the house party was sitting down to tea in the hall. A rapid survey of the guests as the footman helped him out of his coat convinced him that, with the exception of Latter, he didn't know a soul: a second glance indicated that he could contemplate the fact with equanimity. They were a stodgy-looking crowd, and after a brief look he turned his attention to his hostess.

"Where is Lady Manton?" he asked the footman.

"Pouring out tea, sir," returned the man, surprised.

"Great Scott!" said Drummond, aghast. "I've come to the wrong house."

"The wrong house, sir?" echoed the footman, and the sound of their voices made Lady Manton look up.

In an instant that astute woman spotted what had happened. The writer of the strange letter she had received at lunch-time had arrived, and had realized his mistake. Moreover, this was the moment for which she had been waiting ever since, and now to add joy to joy it had occurred when her whole party was assembled to hear every word of her conversation with Drummond. With suitable gratitude she realized that such opportunities are rare.

With a charming smile she advanced towards him, as he stood hesitating by the door.

"Mr. Drummond?" she inquired.

"Yes," he murmured, with a puzzled frown. "But—but I seem to have made some absurd mistake."

She laughed and drew him into the hall.

"A perfectly natural one, I assure you," she replied, speaking so that her guests could hear. "It must have been my sister-in-law that you met at Wiltshire Towers. My husband was not very fit at the time and so I had to refuse the Duchess's invitation." She was handing him a cup of tea as she spoke. "But, of course, I know your cousin, Lord Staveley, well. So we really know one another after all, don't we?"

"Charming of you to put it that way, Lady Manton," answered Drummond, with his infectious grin. "At the same time I feel a bit of an interloper—what! Sort of case of fools toddling in where angels fear to tread."

34

"A somewhat infelicitous quotation," remarked an unctuous-looking man with side whiskers, deprecatingly.

"Catches you too, does it, old bird?" boomed Hugh, putting down his empty cup.

"It was the second part of your quotation that I was alluding to," returned the other acidly, when Lady Manton intervened.

"Of course, Mr. Drummond, my husband and I insist on your remaining with us until you have completed your business in Sheffield."

"Extraordinarily kind of you both, Lady Manton," answered Hugh.

"How long do you think you will be?"

"Three or four days. Perhaps a little more." As he spoke he looked quite casually at Latter. For some minutes that worthy pillar of Parliament had been staring at him with a puzzled frown: now he gave a slight start as recognition came to him. This was the enormous individual who had snored in Sir Bryan Johnstone's office the previous afternoon. Evidently somebody connected with the police, reflected Mr. Latter, and glancing at Drummond's vast size he began to feel more reassured than he had for some time. A comforting sort of individual to have about the premises in the event of a brawl: good man—Sir Bryan. This man looked large enough to cope even with that monstrous black apparition, the thought of which still brought a shudder to his spine.

Drummond was still looking at him, but there was no trace of recognition in his eyes. Evidently they were to meet as strangers before the house-party: quite right, too, when some of the guests themselves might even be members of this vile gang.

"It depends on circumstances outside my control," Drummond was saying. "But if you can do with me for a few days..."

"As long as you like, Mr. Drummond," answered Lady Manton. "And now let me introduce you to my guests."

*****

It was not until just before dinner that Mr. Latter had an opportunity of a few private words with Drummond. They met in the hall, and for a moment no one else was within earshot.

"You were in Sir Bryan Johnstone's office yesterday," said the M.P. hoarsely. "Are you connected with the police?"

"Intimately," answered Hugh. "Even now, Mr. Latter, you are completely surrounded by devoted men who are watching and guarding you."

A gratified smile spread over the other's face, though Drummond's remained absolutely expressionless.

"And how did you get here, Mr. Drummond?"

"By car," returned Hugh gravely.

"I mean into the house party," said Mr. Latter stiffly.

"Ah!" Hugh looked mysterious. "That is between you and me, Mr. Latter."

"Quite: quite. I am discretion itself."

"Until two hours ago I thought I was the biggest liar in the world: now I know I'm not. Our hostess has me beat to a frazzle."

"What on earth are you talking about?" cried Latter, amazed.

"There are wheels within wheels, Mr. Latter," continued Hugh still more mysteriously. "A network of intrigue surrounds us. But do not be afraid. My orders are never to leave your side."

"Good God, Mr. Drummond, do you mean to say...?"

"I mean to say nothing. Only this one thing I will mention." He laid an impressive hand on Latter's arm. "Be very careful what you say to that man with the mutton-chop whiskers and the face like a sheep."

And the startled M.P. was too occupied staring suspiciously at the worthy Sheffield magnate and pillar of Nonconformity who had just descended the stairs with his hostess to notice a sudden peculiar shaking in Drummond's shoulders as he turned away.

*****

Mr. Charles Latter was not a pleasant specimen of humanity even at the best of times, and that evening he was not at his best. He was frightened to the core of his rotten little soul, and when a constitutional coward is frightened the result is not pretty. His conversational efforts at dinner would have shamed a boy of ten, and though he made one or two feeble efforts to pull himself together, it was no good. Try as he would his mind kept reverting to his own position. Over and over again he went on weighing up the points of the case until his brain was whirling. He tried to make out a mental balance sheet where the stock was represented by his own personal safety, but there was always that one unknown factor which he came up against—the real power of this mysterious gang.

Coming up in the train he had decided to curtail his visit as much as possible. He would carry through what he had been told to do, and then, having pocketed his thousand, he would leave the country for a few months. By that time the police should have settled matters. And he had been very lucky. It had proved easy to find the man Delmorlick, and once he had been found, the other more serious matter had proved easy too. Delmorlick had arranged everything, and had brought three other men to meet him in a private room at one of the smaller hotels.

Like all the Count's schemes, every detail was perfect, and once or twice exclamations of amazement interrupted him as he read on. Every possible eventuality was legislated for, and by the time he had finished reading Delmorlick's eyes were glowing with the enthusiasm of a fanatic.

"Magnificent," he had cried, rising and going to the window. "Another nail in the coffin of Capital. And, by heaven! a big one."

He had stood there, his head covered with a shock of untidy hair, staring with sombre eyes at the street below. And beside him had stood one of the other men. After a while Latter joined them, and he too, for a moment, had looked down into the street where little knots of men lounged round doorways with their hands in their pockets, and the apathy of despair on their faces. A few women here and there mingled with them, but there was no laughing or jesting—only the sullenness of lost hope. The hope that had once been theirs of work and plenty was dead; there was nothing for them to do—they were just units in the vast army of unemployed. Occasionally a man better dressed and more prosperous than the others would detach himself from one group and go to another, where he would hold forth long and earnestly. And his listeners would nod their heads vigorously or laugh sheepishly as he passed on.

For a few moments Delmorlick had watched in silence. Then with a grave earnestness in his voice he had turned to Latter.

"We shall win, Mr. Latter, I tell you. That," with a lean forefinger he pointed to the man outside, "is going on all over England, Scotland, and Ireland. And the fools in London prate of economic laws and inflated currencies. What does an abstract cause matter to those men; they want food."

He had glanced at Delmorlick, to find the eyes of the other man fixed on him gravely. He had hardly noticed it at the time—he had been too anxious to get away; now, as he sat at dinner, he found strangely enough that it was the other man's face which seemed to have made the biggest impression on his mind. A new arrival in the place, so Delmorlick had told him—but red-hot for the cause of freedom and anarchy.

He made some vague remark to his neighbour and once more relapsed into moody silence. So far, so good; his job was done—he could leave to-morrow. He would have left that afternoon but for the fact that he had sent his baggage up to Drayton House, and it would have looked strange. But he had already arranged for a wire to be sent to him from London the following morning, and for the night—well, there were Drummond and the police. Decidedly, on points he appeared to be in a winning position—quite a comfortable position. And yet—that unknown factor.... Still, there was always Drummond; the only trouble was that he couldn't quite place him. What on earth had he meant before dinner? He glanced across the table at him now: he was eating salted almonds and making love to his hostess.

"A fool," reflected Mr. Latter, "but a powerful fool. If it was necessary, he'd swallow anything I told him."

And so, towards the end of dinner, aided possibly by his host's very excellent vintage port, Mr. Charles Latter had more or less soothed his fears. Surely he was safe in the house, and nothing would induce him to leave it until he went to the station next morning. No thought of the abominable crime he had planned only that afternoon disturbed his equanimity; as has been said, he was not a pleasant specimen of humanity.

Charles Latter was unmoral rather than immoral: he was a constitutional coward with a strong liking for underhand intrigue, and he was utterly and entirely selfish. In his way he was ambitious: he wanted power, but, though in many respects he was distinctly able, he lacked that essential factor—the ability to work for it. He hated work: he wanted easy results. And to obtain lasting results is not easy, as Mr. Latter gradually discovered. A capability for making flashy speeches covered with a veneer of cleverness is an undoubted asset, but it is an asset the value of which has been gauged to a nicety by the men who count. And so as time went on, and the epoch-making day when he had been returned to Parliament faded into the past, Mr. Latter realized himself for what he was—a thing of no account. And the realization was as gall and wormwood to his soul. It is a realization which comes to many men, and it takes them different ways. Some become resigned—some make new and even more futile efforts: some see the humour of it, and some don't. Mr. Latter didn't: he became spiteful. And a spiteful coward is a nasty thing.

It was just about that time that he met Count Zadowa. It was at dinner at a friend's house, and after the ladies had left he found himself sitting next to the hunchback with the strange, piercing eyes. He wasn't conscious of having said very much: he would have been amazed had he been told that within ten minutes this charming foreigner had read his unpleasant little mind like a book, and had reached a certain and quite definite decision. In fact, looking back on the past few months, Mr. Latter was at a loss to account as to how things had reached their present pass. Had he been told when he stood for Parliament, flaunting all the old hackneyed formulæ, that within two years he would be secretly engaged in red-hot Communist work, he would have laughed the idea to scorn. Anarchy, too: a nasty word, but the only one that fitted the bomb outrage in Manchester, which he had himself organized. Sometimes in the night, he used to wake and lie sweating as he thought of that episode....

And gradually it had become worse and worse. Little by little the charming Count Zadowa, realizing that Mr. Latter possessed just those gifts which he could utilize to advantage, had ceased to be charming. There were many advantages in having a Member of Parliament as chief liaison officer.

There had been that first small slip when he signed a receipt for money paid him to address a revolutionary meeting in South Wales during the coal strike. And the receipt specified the service rendered. An unpleasant document in view of the fact that his principal supporters in his constituency were coal-owners. And after that the descent had been rapid.

Not that even now Mr. Latter felt any twinges of conscience: all he felt was occasional twinges of fear that he might be found out. He was running with the hare and hunting with the hounds with a vengeance, and at times his cowardly little soul grew sick within him. And then, like a dreaded bolt from the blue, had come the letter of warning from the Black Gang.

Anyway, he reflected, as he turned out his light after getting into bed that night, the police knew nothing of his double life. They were all round him, and there was this big fool in the house.... For a moment his heart stopped beating: was it his imagination or was that the figure of a man standing at the foot of the bed?

The sweat poured off his forehead as he tried to speak: then he sat up in bed, plucking with trembling hands at the collar of his pyjamas. Still the shape stood motionless: he could swear there was something there now—he could see it outlined against the dim light of the window. He reached out fearfully for the switch: fumbled a little, and then with a click the light went on. His sudden scream of fear died half-strangled in his throat: a livid anger took the place of terror. Leaning over the foot of the bed and regarding him with solicitous interest, lounged Hugh Drummond.

"All tucked up and comfy, old bean," cried Drummond cheerfully. "Bed socks full of feet and all that sort of thing?"

"How dare you," spluttered Latter, "how dare you come into my room like this...."

"Tush, tush," murmured Drummond, "don't forget my orders, old Latter, my lad. To watch over you as a crooning mother crooneth over the last batch of twins. By the way, my boy, you skimped your teeth pretty badly to-night. You'll have to do better to-morrow. Most of your molars must be sitting up and begging for Kolynos if that's your normal effort."

"Do you mean to tell me that you were in here while I was undressing," said Latter angrily. "You exceed your instructions, sir: and I shall report your unwarrantable impertinence to Sir Bryan Johnstone when I return to London."

"Exactly, Mr. Latter. But when will you return to London?" Drummond regarded him dispassionately. "To put some, if not all, of the cards on the table, the anonymous letter of warning which you received was not quite so anonymous as you would have liked. In other words, you know exactly whom it came from."

"I don't," replied the other. "I know that it came from an abominable gang who have been committing a series of outrages lately. And that is why I applied for police protection."

"Quite so, Mr. Latter. And as—er—Fate would have it, I am here to help carry out that rôle."

"What did you mean when you gave me that warning before dinner? That man is one of the leading citizens of Sheffield."

"That was just a little jest, Mr. Latter, to amuse you during the evening. The danger does not lie there."

"Where does it lie?"

"Probably where you least expect it," returned Drummond with an enigmatic smile.

"I shall be going to-morrow," said Latter with attempted nonchalance. "Until then I rely on you."

"Precisely," murmured Drummond. "So you have completed your business here quicker than you anticipated."

"Yes. To be exact, this afternoon before you arrived."

"And was that the business which brought you to Sheffield?"

"Principally. Though I really don't understand this catechism, Mr. Drummond. And now I wish to go to sleep...."

39

"I'm afraid you can't, Mr. Latter. Not quite yet." For a moment or two Charles Latter stared at the imperturbable face at the foot of his bed: it seemed to him that a strange tension was creeping into the conversation—a something he could not place which made him vaguely alarmed.

"Do you think this mysterious Black Gang would approve of your business this afternoon?" asked Drummond quietly.

Mr. Latter started violently.

"How should I know of what the scoundrels would approve?" he cried angrily. "And anyway, they can know nothing about it."

"You feel quite confident in Mr. Delmorlick's discretion with regard to the friends he selects?"

And now a pulse was beginning to hammer in Mr. Latter's throat, and his voice when he spoke was thick and unnatural.

"How do you know anything about Delmorlick?"

Drummond smiled. "May I reply by asking a similar question, Mr. Latter? How do you?"

"I met him this afternoon on political business," stammered the other, staring fascinated at the man opposite, from whose face all trace of buffoonery seemed to have vanished, to be replaced by a grim sternness the more terrifying because it was so utterly unexpected. And he had thought Drummond a fool....

"Would it be indiscreet to inquire the nature of the business?"

"Yes," muttered Latter. "It was private."

"That I can quite imagine," returned Drummond grimly. "But since you're so reticent I will tell you. This afternoon you made arrangements, perfect in every detail, to blow up the main power station of the Greystone works." The man in the bed started violently. "The result of that would have been to throw some three thousand men out of work for at least a couple of months."

"It's a lie," said Latter thickly.

"Your object in so doing was obvious," continued Drummond. "Money. I don't know how much, and I didn't know who from—until last night." And now Latter was swallowing hard, and clutching the bedclothes with hands that shook like leaves.

"You saw me last night, Mr. Latter, didn't you? And I found out your headquarters...."

"In God's name—who are you?" His voice rose almost to a scream. "Aren't you the police?"

"No—I am not." He was coming nearer, and Latter cowered back, mouthing. "I am not the police, you wretched thing: I am the leader of the Black Gang."

Latter felt the other's huge hands on him, and struggled like a puny child, whimpering, half sobbing. He writhed and squirmed as a gag was forced into his mouth: then he felt a rope cut his wrists as they were lashed behind his back. And all the while the other went on speaking in a calm, leisurely voice.

"The leader of the Black Gang, Mr. Latter: the gang that came into existence to exterminate things like you. Ever since the war you poisonous reptiles have been at work stirring up internal trouble in this country. Not one in ten of you believe what you preach: your driving force is money and your own advancement. And as for your miserable dupes—those priceless fellows who follow you blindly because—God help them, they're hungry and their wives are hungry—what do you care for them, Mr. Latter? You just laugh in your sleeve and pocket the cash."

With a heave he jerked the other on to the floor, and proceeded to lash him to the foot of the bed.

"I have had my eye on you, Mr. Latter, since the Manchester effort when ten men were killed, and you were the murderer. But other and more important matters have occupied my time. You see, my information is very good—better than Delmorlick's selection of friends. The new devoted adherent to your cause this afternoon happens to be an intimate personal friend of mine."

He was busying himself with something that he had taken from his pocket—a thick, square slab with a hole in the centre.

"I admit that your going to the police with my note surprised me. And it really was extraordinarily lucky that I happened to be in the office at the time. But it necessitated a slight change of plan on my part. If dear old McIver and his minions are outside the house, it's much simpler for me to be in. And now, Mr. Latter—to come to business."

He stood in front of the bound man, whose eyes were rolling horribly.

"We believe in making the punishment fit the crime. This afternoon you planned to destroy the livelihood of several thousand men with explosive, simply that you might make money. Here," he held up the square slab, "is a pound of the actual gun-cotton, which was removed from Delmorlick himself before he started on a journey to join my other specimens. I propose to place this slab under you, Mr. Latter, and to light this piece of fuse which is attached to it. The fuse will take about three minutes to burn. During that three minutes if you can get free, so much the better for you; if not—well, it would be a pity not to have any explosion at all in Sheffield, wouldn't it?"

For a moment or two Drummond watched the struggling, terrified man, and his eyes were hard and merciless. Then he went to the door, and Latter heard it opened and shut, and moaned horribly. His impotent struggles increased: out of the corner of his eye he could see the fire burning nearer and nearer. And then all of a sudden something seemed to snap in his brain....

Four minutes later Drummond came out from the screen behind which he had been standing. He picked up the burnt-out fuse and the block of wood to which it had been attached. Then he undid the ropes that bound the other man, removed the gag and put him back into bed. And after a while he nodded thoughtfully.

"Poetic justice," he murmured. "And it saves a lot of trouble."

Then, after one searching look round the room, he turned out the light and stepped quietly into the passage.

*****

"An extraordinary thing, McIver," said Sir Bryan Johnstone, late on the afternoon of the following day. "You say that when you saw Mr. Latter this morning he was mad."

"Mad as a hatter, sir," answered McIver, turning for confirmation to Drummond, who was sprawling in a chair.

"Absolutely up the pole, Tum-tum," agreed Drummond.

"Gibbered like a fool," said McIver, "and struggled wildly whenever he got near the foot of the bed. Seemed terrified of it, somehow. Did you notice that, Mr. Drummond?"

"My dear old lad, it was only ten o'clock, and I was barely conscious," yawned that worthy, lighting a cigarette.

"Well, anyway, you had no trouble with the gang, McIver," said his chief.

"None, sir," agreed the Inspector. "I thought they wouldn't try it on with me twice. I heard some fool story just before I caught the train, about one of the night watchmen at a big works who swears he saw a sort of court-martial—he was an old soldier—being held on three men by a lot of black-masked figures. But a lot of these people have got this yarn on the brain, Sir Bryan. It's spread a good deal further than I thought."

Sir Bryan nodded thoughtfully.

"I must say I'd like to know what sent Charles Latter mad!"

Drummond sat up lazily.

"Good heavens! Tumkins, don't you know? The house-party, old son—the house-party; they had to be seen to be believed."

6

In which an effusion is sent to the newspapers

Take a garrulous night-watchman and an enterprising journalist; mix them together over one, or even two glasses of beer, and a hard-worked editor feels safe for a column every time. And since the night-watchman at Greystone's Steel Works was very garrulous, and the journalist was young and ambitious, the result produced several columns of the sort of stuff that everybody likes to read, and pretends he doesn't.

Mr. Day was the night-watchman's name, and Mr. Day was prepared to tell his story at a pint a time to anyone who cared to listen. It differed in detail, the difference depending entirely on the number of payments received during the day, but the essential part remained the same. And it was that essential part that was first published in one of the local Sheffield papers, and from there found its way into the London press.

Mr. Day, it appeared, had, according to his usual custom, been making his hourly tour of the works. It was about midnight, or perhaps a little after, that he thought he heard the sound of voices coming from the central power station. As he approached it had seemed to him that it was more lit up than it had been on his previous round, when only one electric light had been burning. He was on the point of opening the door to go in and investigate, when he heard at least half a dozen voices speaking angrily, and one in particular had stood out above the others. It was loud and convulsed with passion, and on hearing it Mr. Day, remembering his wife and four children, had paused.

"You damned traitor, as sure as there's a God above, I'll kill you for this some day."

Such were the words which it appeared had given Mr. Day cause for reflection. At any time, and in any place, they would be apt to stand out from the ordinary level of bright chat; but as Mr. Day remarked succinctly, "they fair gave me the creeps, coming out o' that there place, which was hempty, mind you, not 'alf an hour before."

And there are few, I think, who can blame him for his decision not to open the door, but to substitute for such a course a strategic move to a flank. There was an outside flight of steps leading to a door which opened on to the upstairs platform where stood the indicator board. And half-way up that flight of stairs was a window—a window through which Mr. Day was peering a few seconds afterwards.

It was at this point in the narrative that Mr. Day was wont to pause, while his listeners drew closer. Standing between the four huge dynamos which supplied the whole of the power necessary for the works were ten or a dozen men. Three of them had their hands lashed behind their backs, and these were the only three whose faces he could see. The others—and here came a still more impressive pause—were completely covered in black from head to foot. Black masks—black cloaks, the only difference between them being in height. He couldn't hear what was being said: ever since the Boer War Mr. Day had been a little hard of hearing. But what it reminded him of was a drum-head court-martial. The three men whose hands were lashed behind them were the prisoners; the men in black, standing motionless round them, their judges. He heard vaguely the sound of a voice which went on speaking for some time. And since the three bound men seemed to be staring at one of the masked figures, he concluded that that must be the speaker. Then he saw the masked men surround the other three closely, and when they stood back again Mr. Day noticed that the prisoners had been gagged as well as bound. It was at this moment, apparently, that a hazy idea of going for the police penetrated his brain for the first time, but it was too late. Powerless in the hands of their captors, the three men were forced to the door, and shortly afterwards Mr. Day affirmed that he heard the sound of a car driving off. But he was unable to swear to it; he was still flattening a fascinated nose against the window; for two of the masked men had remained behind, and Mr. Day wasn't going to miss anything.

These two gathered together into bundles a lot of things that looked like wooden slabs—also some stuff that looked like black cord. Then they walked carefully round the whole power station, as if to make sure that nothing had been left behind. Apparently satisfied with their inspection, they went to the door, carrying the bundles they had collected. They turned out all the lights except the one which had originally been burning, took one final look round to make certain that everything was as it should be, and then they, too, vanished into the night, leaving Mr. Day to scratch his head and wonder if he had been dreaming.

In fact, but for one indisputable certainty, it is very doubtful whether Mr. Day's story would have been received with the respect which it undoubtedly deserved. When he first recounted it there were scoffers of the most incredulous type; scoffers who cast the most libellous reflections on the manner in which Mr. Day had spent the evening before going on duty, and it was not until the fact became established two or three days later that three men who should have come to work the next morning at their different jobs not only failed to appear, but had completely disappeared, leaving no trace behind them, that the scoffers became silent. Moreover, the enterprising journalist came on the scene, and Mr. Day became famous, and Mr. Day developed an infinite capacity for beer. Was not he, wildly improbable though his story might be, the only person who could throw any light at all on the mysterious disappearance of three workmen from Sheffield? Certainly the journalist considered he was, and proceeded to write a column of the most convincing journalese to proclaim his belief to the world at large, and Sheffield in particular.

Thus was the ball started. And no sooner had it commenced to move, than it received astonishing impetus from all sorts of unexpected directions. The journalist, in his search for copy to keep his infant alive, discovered to his astonishment that he had unearthed a full-grown child. The activities of the Black Gang were not such a profound mystery as he had at first thought. And though he failed to get the slightest clue as to the identity of the men composing it, he was soon absolutely convinced of the truth of Mr. Day's story. But there he stuck; the whole matter became one of conjecture in his mind. That there was a Black Gang, he was certain; but why or wherefore was beyond him.

Men he encountered in odd places were noncommittal. Some obviously knew nothing about it; others shrugged their shoulders and looked wise.

There was one group of youngish men he approached on the matter. They were standing at the corner of the long street which led from Greystone's works, muttering together, and their conversation ceased abruptly as he sauntered up.

"Journalist, are you?" said one. "Want to know about this 'ere Black Gang? Well, look 'ere, mister, I'll tell you one thing. See them furnaces over there?"

He pointed to the ruddy, orange light of Greystone's huge furnaces, glowing fiercely against the evening sky.

"Well, if me and my mates ever catch the leader of that there gang, or anybody wot's connected with it, they goes in them furnaces alive."

"Shut up, yer blasted fool!" cried one of the others.

"Think I'm afraid of that bunch!" snarled the first speaker. "A bunch wot's frightened to show their faces..."

But the journalist had passed on.

"Don't you pay no attention to them young fools, mate," said an elderly, quiet-looking man, who was standing smoking in a doorway a few yards on. "They talks too much and they does too little."

"I was asking them about this so-called Black Gang," said the searcher after news.

"Ah!" The elderly man spat thoughtfully. "Don't profess to know nothing about them myself; but if wot I've 'eard is true, we could do with a few more like 'em."

And once more the journalist passed on.

The police refused point-blank to make any communications on the matter at all. They had heard Mr. Day's story, and while not disposed to dismiss it entirely, they would not say that they were prepared to accept it completely; and since it was a jolly day outside, and they were rather busy, the door was along the passage to the left.

Such were the ingredients, then, with which one, and sometimes two columns daily were made up for the edification of the inhabitants of Sheffield. Brief notices appeared in one or two of the London dailies, coupled with the announcement that Mr. Charles Latter had suffered a nervous breakdown, and that this well-known M.P. had gone to a nursing-home for some weeks. But beyond that the matter was too local to be of importance, until a sudden dramatic development revived the flagging interest in Sheffield, and brought the matter into the national limelight.

It was nothing more or less than an announcement purporting to come from the leader of the Black Gang himself, and sent to the editor of the Sheffield paper. It occupied a prominent position in the centre page, and was introduced to the public in the following words:

"The following communication has been received by the editor. The original, which he has handed over to the proper authorities, was typewritten; the postmark was a London one. The editor offers no comment on the genuineness of the document, beyond stating that it is printed exactly as it was received."

The document ran as follows:

"In view of the conflicting rumours started by the story of Mr. Day, the night-watchman at Greystone's works, it may be of interest to the public to know that his story is true in every detail. The three men whom he saw bound were engaged at the instigation of others in an attempt to wreck the main power station, thereby largely increasing unemployment in Sheffield, and fomenting more unrest. The driving force behind this, as behind other similar activities, is international. The source of it all lies in other countries; the object is the complete ruin of the great sober majority of workers in England by a loud-voiced, money-seeking minority which is composed of unscrupulous scoundrels and fanatical madmen. For these apostles of anarchy a home has been prepared, where the doctrines of Communism are strictly enforced. The three men who have disappeared from Sheffield have gone to that home, but there is still plenty of room for others. Mr. Charles Latter has gone mad, otherwise he would have accompanied them. The more intelligent the man, the more vile the scoundrel. Charles Latter was intelligent. There are others more intelligent than he. It is expressly for their benefit that the Black Gang came into being. (Signed) THE LEADER OF THE GANG."

The reception of this remarkable document was mixed. On the strength of the first sentence Mr. Day's price rose to two pints; but it was the rest of the communication which aroused public interest. For the first time some tangible reason had been advanced to account for the presence of the three bound men and their masked captors in the power-station at Greystones. Inquiries revealed the fact that all three of them were men educated above the average, and of very advanced Socialistic views. And to that extent the document seemed credible. But it was the concluding sentences that baffled the public.

True, Mr. Charles Latter, M.P., had been staying on the night in question at Lady Manton's house a few miles out of the town. Equally true he had had a nervous breakdown which necessitated his removal to a nursing-home in London. But what connection there could possibly be between him and the three men it was difficult to see. It was most positively asserted that the well-known Member of Parliament had not left Drayton House during the night on which the affair took place; and yet, if credence was to be attached to the document, there was an intimate connection between him and the affair at the steel works. Callers at the nursing-home came away none the wiser; his doctor had positively forbidden a soul to be admitted save his brother, who came away frowning after the first visit, and returned no more. For Charles Latter not only had not recognized him, but had shrunk away, babbling nonsense, while continually his eyes had sought the foot of the bed with a look of dreadful terror in them.

And so speculation continued. No further communication emanated from the mysterious Black Gang. Mr. Latter was insane; the three men had disappeared, and Mr. Day, even at two pints, could say no more than he had said already. There were people who dismissed the entire thing as an impudent and impertinent hoax, and stated that the editor of the Sheffield paper should be prosecuted for libel. It was obvious, they explained, what had occurred. Some irresponsible practical joker had, for reasons of his own, connected together the two acts, whose only real connection was that they had occurred about the same time, and had maliciously sent the letter to the paper.

But there were others who were not so sure—people who nodded wisely at one another from the corners of trains, and claimed inside knowledge of strange happenings unknown to the mere public. They affirmed darkly that there was more in it than met the eye, and relapsed into confidential mutterings.

And then, when nothing further happened, the matter died out of the papers, and speculation ceased amongst the public. The general impression left behind favoured a hoax; and at that it was allowed to remain until the events occurred which were to prove that it was a very grim reality.

*****

But whatever the general public may have thought about the matter, there were two people in London who viewed the sudden newspaper notoriety with rage and anger. And it is, perhaps, needless to say that neither of them concurred in the impression that it was a hoax; only too well did they know that it was nothing of the kind.

The first of these was Count Zadowa, alias Mr. William Atkinson. He had duly received from Latter a telegram in code stating that everything was well—a telegram despatched from Sheffield after the meeting with Delmorlick in the afternoon. And from that moment he had heard nothing. The early editions of the evening papers on the following day had contained no reference to any explosion at Sheffield; the later ones had announced Mr. Latter's nervous breakdown. And the Count, reading between the lines, had wondered, though at that time he was far from guessing the real truth. Then had come strange rumours—rumours which resulted in the summoning post-haste from Sheffield of a man who was alluded to in the archives at 5, Green Street, as John Smith, commission agent. And, though he may have fully deserved the description of commission agent, a glance at his face gave one to wonder at his right to the name of John Smith.

"Tell me exactly what has happened," said the Count, quietly, pointing to a chair in his inner office. "Up to date I have only heard rumours."

And John Smith, with the accent of a Polish Jew, told. Mr. Latter had called on him, early in the afternoon, and, in accordance with his instructions, he had arranged a meeting between Mr. Latter and Delmorlick at an hotel. Delmorlick had taken three other men with him, and he presumed everything had been arranged at that meeting. No; he had not been present himself. For two of Delmorlick's companions he could vouch; in fact—and then, for the first time, Count Zadowa heard the story so ably spread abroad by Mr. Day. For it was those two men and Delmorlick who had disappeared.

"Then it was the fourth man who gave it away," snapped the Count. "Who was he?"

"He called himself Jackson," faltered the other. "But I haven't seen him since."

Thoughtfully the Count beat a tattoo with his fingers on the desk in front of him; no one looking at him would have guessed for an instant the rage that was seething in his brain. For the first time he realized fully that, perfect though his own organization might be, he had come up against one that was still better.

"And what about this nervous breakdown of Mr. Latter's?" he demanded at length.

But on that subject John Smith knew nothing. He had no ideas on the subject, and, after a few searching questions, he found himself curtly dismissed, leaving the Count to ponder over the knotty point as to the connection between Latter's breakdown and the affair at the power station. And he was still pondering over it three days later when the bombshell exploded in the form of the document to the Press. That the concluding sentences were evidently directed against him did not worry him nearly as much as the publicity afforded to activities in which secrecy was essential. And what worried him even more was the fact that others on the Continent—men whose names were never mentioned, but who regarded him almost as he regarded Latter—would see the English papers, and would form their own conclusions. Already some peremptory letters had reached him, stating that the activities of the Black Gang must cease—how, it was immaterial. And he had replied stating that he had the thing well in hand. On top of which had come this damnable document, which was published in practically every paper in the country, and had produced a sort of silly-season discussion from "Retired Colonel" and "Maiden Lady." Of no importance to him that "Common Sense" decreed that it was a stupid hoax: he knew it was not. And so did those others, as he very soon found out. Two days after the appearance of the document, he received a letter which bore the postmark of Amsterdam. It stated merely: "I am coming," and was signed X. And had anyone been present when Count Zadowa opened that letter in his private office, he would have seen an unexpected sight. He would have seen him tear the letter into a thousand pieces, and then wipe his forehead with a hand that trembled a little. For Count Zadowa, who terrified most men, was frightened himself.

The second person who viewed this sudden notoriety with dislike was Inspector McIver. And in his case, too, the reason was largely personal. He was caught on the horns of a dilemma, as Sir Bryan Johnstone, who was not too pleased with the turn of events, pointed out to him a little caustically. Either the entire thing was a hoax, in which case, why had McIver himself taken such elaborate precautions to prevent anything happening? or it was not a hoax, in which case McIver had been made a complete fool of.

"I'll stake my reputation on the fact that no one got into or left the house that night, Sir Bryan," he reiterated again and again. "That the Black Gang was at work in the town, I admit; but I do not believe that Mr. Latter's condition is anything more than a strange coincidence."

It was an interview that he had with Mr. Latter's brother, that caused him to go round to Drummond's house in Brook Street. Much as he disliked having to do so he felt he must leave no stone unturned if he was to get to the bottom of the affair, and Mr. Latter's brother had said one or two things which he thought might be worth following up. If only Hugh Drummond wasn't such a confounded fool, he reflected savagely, as he turned into Bond Street, it would have been possible to get some sane information. But that was his chief's fault; he entirely washed his hands of the responsibility of roping in such a vast idiot. And it was at that stage in his meditations that a Rolls-Royce drew silently up beside him, and the cheerful voice of the subject of his thoughts hailed him delightedly.

"The very man, and the very spot!"

McIver turned round and nodded briefly.

"Morning, Captain Drummond! I was just going round to your house to see you."

"But, my dear old top," cried Hugh, "don't you see where you are? The portals of the Regency positively beckon us. Behind those portals, a cocktail apiece, and you shall tell me all your troubles."

He gently propelled the inspector through the doors of the celebrated club, still babbling cheerfully.

"After profound experience, old lad," he remarked, coming to anchor by the bar, "I have come to the conclusion that there is only one thing in this world better than having a cocktail at twelve o'clock."

"What's that?" said McIver perfunctorily.

"Having two," answered Drummond triumphantly.

The inspector smiled wanly. After his profound experience he had come to the conclusion that there could exist no bigger ass in the world than Drummond, but he followed a trade where at times it is necessary to suffer fools gladly. And this was one of them.

"Is there any place where we could have a little private talk, Captain Drummond?" he asked, as the other pushed a Martini towards him.

"What about that corner over there?" said Drummond, after glancing round the room.

"Excellent!" agreed the inspector, and, picking up his cocktail, he crossed over to it and sat down. It took his host nearly five minutes to do the same short journey, and McIver chafed irritably at the delay. He was a busy man, and it seemed to him that Drummond knew everyone in the room. Moreover, he insisted on talking to them at length. And once again a feeling of anger against his chief filled his mind. What had Drummond except his great strength to distinguish him from this futile crowd of cocktail-drinking men? All of them built on the same pattern; all of them fashioned along the same lines. Talking a strange jargon of their own—idle, perfectly groomed, bored. As far as they were concerned, he was non-existent save as the man who was with Drummond. He smiled a little grimly; he, who did more man's work in a week than the whole lot of them put together got through in a year. A strange caste, he reflected, as he sipped his drink; a caste which does not aim at, because it essentially is, good form; a caste which knows only one fetish—the absolute repression of all visible emotion; a caste which incidentally pulled considerably more than its own weight in the war. McIver gave them credit for that.

"Sorry to be so long." Drummond lowered himself into a chair. "The place is always crowded at this hour. Now, what's the little worry?"

"It's about the affair up at Sheffield," said the inspector. "I suppose you've seen this communication in the papers, purporting to come from the leader of the Black Gang."

"Rather, old lad," answered Drummond. "Waded through it over the eggs the other morning. Pretty useful effort, I thought."

"The public at large regard it as a hoax," continued McIver. "Now, I know it isn't! The typewriter used in the original document is the same as was used in their previous communications."

"By Jove, that's quick!" said Drummond admiringly. "Deuced quick."

McIver frowned.

"Now please concentrate, Captain Drummond. The concluding sentence of the letter would lead one to suppose that there was some connection between the activities of this gang and Mr. Charles Latter's present condition. I, personally, don't believe it. I think it was mere coincidence. But whichever way it is, I would give a great deal to know what sent him mad."

"Is he absolutely up the pole?" demanded Drummond.

"Absolutely! His brother has seen him, and after he had seen him he came to me. He tells me that the one marked symptom is an overmastering terror of something which he seems to see at the foot of the bed. He follows this thing round with his eyes—I suppose he thinks it's coming towards him—and then he screams. His brother believes that someone or something must have been in his room that night—a something so terrifying that it sent him mad. To my mind, of course, the idea is wildly improbable, but strange things do occur."

"Undoubtedly!" agreed Drummond.

"Now you were in the house," went on the inspector; "you even examined his room, as you told Sir Bryan. Now, did you examine it closely?"

"Even to looking under the bed," answered Drummond brightly.

"And there was nothing there? No place where anybody or anything could hide?"

"Not a vestige of a spot. In fact, my dear old police hound," continued Drummond, draining his glass, "if the genial brother is correct in his supposition the only conclusion we can come to is that I sent him mad myself."

McIver frowned again.

"I wish you'd be serious, Captain Drummond. There are other things in life beside cocktails and—this." He waved an expressive hand round the room. "The matter is an important one. You can give me no further information? You heard no sounds during the night?"

"Only the sheep-faced man snoring," answered Drummond, with a grin. And then, of a sudden, he became serious, and leaning across the table, he stared fixedly at the inspector.

"I think we must conclude, McIver, that the madness of Mr. Latter is due to the ghosts of the past, and perhaps the spectres of the present. A punishment, McIver, for things done which it is not good to do—a punishment which came to him in the night. That's when the ghosts are abroad." He noted McIver's astonished face and gradually his own relaxed into a smile. "Pretty good, that—wasn't it, after only one cocktail. You ought to hear me after my third."

"Thanks very much, Captain Drummond," laughed the inspector, "but that was quite good enough for me. We don't deal in ghosts in my service."

"Well, I've done my best," sighed Drummond, waving languidly at a waiter to repeat the dose. "It's either that or me. I know my face is pretty bad, but——"

"I don't think we need worry about either alternative," said McIver, rising.

"Right oh, old lad," answered Drummond. "You know best. You'll have another?"

"No more, thanks. I have to work sometimes."

The inspector picked up his hat and stick, and Drummond strolled across the room with him.

"Give my love to Tum-tum."

"Sir Bryan is not at the office to-day, Captain Drummond," answered McIver coldly. "Good-morning."

With a faint smile Drummond watched the square, sturdy figure swing through the doors into Bond Street, then he turned and thoughtfully made his way back to the table.

"Make it seven, instead of two," he told the waiter, who was hovering round.

And had McIver returned at that moment he would have seen six of these imperturbable, bored men rise unobtrusively from different parts of the room, and saunter idly across to the corner where he had recently been sitting. It would probably not have struck him as an unusual sight—Drummond and six of his pals having a second drink; in fact, it would have struck him as being very usual. He was an unimaginative man was the inspector.

"Well," said Peter Darrell, lighting a cigarette. "And what had he got to say?"

"Nothing of interest," answered Drummond. "I told him the truth, and he wouldn't believe me. Algy back yet?"

"This morning," said Ted Jerningham. "He's coming round here. Had a bit of trouble, I gather. And, talk of the devil—here he is."

Algy Longworth, his right arm in a sling, was threading his way towards them.

"What's happened, Algy?" said Hugh as he came up.

"That firebrand Delmorlick stuck a knife into me," grinned Algy. "We put him on a rope and dropped him overboard, and towed him for three hundred yards. Cooled his ardour. I think he'll live all right."

"And how are all the specimens?"

"Prime, old son—prime! If we leave 'em long enough, they'll all have murdered one another."

Drummond put down his empty glass with a laugh.

"The first British Soviet. Long life to 'em! Incidentally, ten o'clock to-night. Usual rendezvous. In view of your arm, Algy—transfer your instructions to Ted. You've got 'em?"

"In my pocket here. But, Hugh, I can easily——"

"Transfer to Ted, please. No argument! We've got a nice little job—possibly some sport. Read 'em, Ted—and business as usual. So long, boys! Phyllis and I are lunching with some awe-inspiring relatives."

The group broke up as casually as it had formed, only Ted Jerningham remaining behind. And he was reading what looked like an ordinary letter. He read it through carefully six or seven times; then he placed it in the fire, watching it until it was reduced to ashes. A few minutes later he was sitting down to lunch with his father, Sir Patrick Jerningham, Bart., at the latter's club in Pall Mall. And it is possible that that worthy and conscientious gentleman would not have eaten such a hearty meal had he known that his only son was detailed for a job that very night which, in the event of failure, would mean either prison or a knife in the back—probably the latter.

7

In which a bomb bursts at unpleasantly close quarters

It was perhaps because the thought of failure never entered Hugh Drummond's head that such a considerable measure of success had been possible up to date—that, and the absolute, unquestioning obedience which he demanded of his pals, and which they accorded him willingly. As they knew, he laid no claims to brilliance; but as they also knew, he hid a very shrewd commonsense beneath his frivolous manner. And having once accepted the sound military truism that one indifferent general is better than two good ones, they accepted his leadership with unswerving loyalty. What was going to be the end of their self-imposed fight against the pests of society did not worry them greatly; all that mattered was that there should be a certain amount of sport in the collection of the specimens. Granted the promise of that, they willingly sacrificed any engagements and carried out Hugh's orders to the letter. Up to date, however, the campaign, though far from being dull, had not produced any really big results. A number of sprats and a few moderate-sized fish had duly been caught in the landing-net, and been sent to the private pool to meditate at leisure. But nothing really large had come their way. Zaboleff was a good haul, and the madness of Mr. Latter was all for the national welfare. But the Black Gang, which aimed merely at the repression of terrorism by terrorism, had found it too easy. The nauseating cowardice of the majority of their opponents was becoming monotonous, their strong aversion to soap and water, insanitary. They wanted big game—not the rats that emerged from the sewers.

Even Drummond had begun to feel that patriotism might be carried too far, until the moment when the address in Hoxton had fallen into his hands. Then, with the optimism that lives eternal in the hunter's breast, fresh hope had arisen in his mind. It had been held in abeyance temporarily owing to the little affair at Sheffield. Yet now that that was over he had determined on a bigger game. If it failed—if they drew blank—he had almost decided to chuck the thing up altogether. Phyllis, he knew, would be overjoyed if he did.

"Just this one final coup, old girl," he said, as they sat waiting in the Carlton for the awe-inspiring relatives. "I've got it cut and dried, and it comes off to-night. If it's a dud, we'll dissolve ourselves—at any rate, for the present. If only——"

He sighed, and his wife looked at him reproachfully.

"I know you want another fight with Peterson, you old goat," she remarked. "But you'll never see him again, or that horrible girl."

"Don't you think I shall, Phyl?" He stared despondently at his shoes. "I can't help feeling myself that somewhere or other behind all this that cheery bird is lurking. My dear, it would be too ghastly if I never saw him again."

"The next time you see him, Hugh," she answered quietly, "he won't take any chances with you."

"But, my angel child," he boomed cheerfully. "I don't want him to. Not on your life! Nor shall I. Good Lord! Here they are. Uncle Timothy looks more like a mangel-wurzel than ever."

And so at nine-thirty that evening, a party of five men sat waiting in a small sitting-room, of a house situated in a remote corner of South Kensington. Some easels stood round the walls covered with half-finished sketches, as befitted a room belonging to a budding artist such as Toby Sinclair Not that he was an artist or even a budding one, but he felt that a man must have some excuse for living in South Kensington. And so he had bought the sketches and put them round the room, principally to deceive the landlady. The fact that he was never there except at strange hours merely confirmed that excellent woman's opinion that all artists were dissolute rascals. But he paid his rent regularly, and times were hard, especially in South Kensington. Had the worthy soul known that her second best sitting-room was the rendezvous of this Black Gang whose letter to the paper she and her husband had discussed over the matutinal kipper, it is doubtful if she would have been so complacent. But she didn't know, and continued her weekly dusting of the sketches with characteristic zeal.

"Ted should be here soon," said Drummond, glancing at his watch. "I hope he's got the bird all right."

"You didn't get into the inner room, did you. Hugh?" said Peter Darrell.

"No. But I saw enough to know that it's beyond our form, old lad. We've got to have a skilled cracksman to deal with one of the doors—and almost certainly anything important will be in a safe inside."

"Just run over the orders again." Toby Sinclair came back from drawing the blinds even more closely together.

"Perfectly simple," said Hugh. "Ted and I and Ginger Martin—if he's got him—will go straight into the house through the front door. I know the geography of the place all right, and I've already laid out the caretaker clerk fellow once. Then we must trust to luck. There shouldn't be anybody there except the little blighter of a clerk. The rest of you will hang about outside in case of any trouble. Don't bunch together, keep on the move; but keep the doors in sight. When you see us come out again, make your own way home. Can't give you any more detailed instructions because I don't know what may turn up. I shall rig myself out here, after Ted arrives. You had better go to your own rooms and do it, but wait first to make sure that he's roped in Ginger Martin."

He glanced up as the door opened and Jerry Seymour—sometime of the R.F.C.—put his head into the room.

"Ted's here, and he's got the bird all right. Unpleasant-looking bloke with a flattened face."

"Right." Drummond rose, and crossed to a cupboard. "Clear off, you fellows. Zero—twelve midnight."

From the cupboard he pulled a long black cloak and mask, which he proceeded to put on, while the others disappeared with the exception of Jerry Seymour, who came into the room. He was dressed in livery like a chauffeur, and he had, in fact, been driving the car in which Ted had brought Ginger Martin.

"Any trouble?" asked Drummond.

"No. Once he was certain Ted was nothing to do with the police he came like a bird," said Jerry. "The fifty quid did it." Then he grinned. "You know, Ted's a marvel. I'll defy anybody to recognize him."

Drummond nodded, and sat down at the table facing the door.

"Tell Ted to bring him up. And I don't want him to see you, Jerry, so keep out of the light."

Undoubtedly Jerry Seymour was right with regard to Jerningham's make-up. As he and Martin came into the room, it was only the sudden start and cry on the part of the crook that made Drummond certain as to which was which.

"Blimey!" muttered the man, shrinking back as he saw the huge figure in black confronting him. "Wot's the game, guv'nor?"

"There's no game, Martin," said Drummond reassuringly. "You've been told what you're wanted for, haven't you? A little professional assistance to-night, for which you will be paid fifty pounds, is all we ask of you."

But Ginger Martin still seemed far from easy in his mind. Like most of the underworld he had heard strange stories of the Black Gang long before they had attained the notoriety of print. Many of them were exaggerated, doubtless, but the general impression left in his mind was one of fear. The police were always with him: the police he understood. But this strange gang was beyond his comprehension, and that in itself was sufficient to frighten him.

"You're one of this 'ere Black Gang," he said sullenly, glancing at the door in front of which Jerningham was standing. Should he chance it and make a dash to get away? Fifty pounds are fifty pounds, but—— He gave a little shiver as his eyes came round again to the motionless figure on the other side of the table.

"Quite correct, Martin," said the same reassuring voice. "And it's only because I don't want you to recognize me that I'm dressed up like this. We don't mean you any harm." The voice paused for a moment, and then went on again. "You understand that, Martin. We don't mean you any harm, unless"—and once again there came a pause—"unless you try any monkey tricks. You are to do exactly as I tell you, without question and at once. If you do you will receive fifty pounds. If you don't—well, Martin, I have ways of dealing with people who don't do what I tell them."

There was a silence while Ginger Martin fidgeted about, looking like a trapped animal. How he wished now that he'd had nothing to do with the thing at all. But it was too late to bother about that; here he was, utterly ignorant of his whereabouts—trapped.

"What do you want me to do, guv'nor?" he said at last.

"Open a safe amongst other things," answered Drummond. "Have you brought your tools and things?"

"Yus—I've brought the outfit," muttered the other. "Where is the safe? 'Ere?"

"No, Martin, not here. Some distance away in fact. We shall start in about an hour. Until then you will stop in this room. You can have a whisky-and-soda, and my friend here will stay with you. He has a gun, Martin, so remember what I said. No monkey tricks."

With fascinated eyes the crook watched the speaker rise and cross to an inner door. Standing, he seemed more huge than ever, and Martin gave a sigh of relief as the door closed behind him.

"I reckon 'e wouldn't win a prize as a blinking dwarf," he remarked hoarsely to Jerningham. "I say, mister, wot abaht that there whisky-and-soda?"

*****

The entrance to Number 5, Green Street, proved easier than Drummond had expected—so easy as to be almost suspicious. No lights shone in the windows above: the house seemed completely deserted. Moreover, the door into the street was unbolted, and without a moment's hesitation Drummond opened it and stepped inside, followed by Martin and Ted Jerningham. The long black cloak had been discarded; only the black mask concealed his face, as the three men stood inside the door, listening intently. Not a sound was audible, and after a moment or two Drummond felt his way cautiously through the downstairs office towards the flight of stairs that led to the rooms above. And it was just as his foot was on the first stair that a sudden noise behind him made him draw back sharply into the darkness behind the counter, with a warning whisper to the other two to follow his example.

The front door had opened again; someone else had come in. They could see nothing, and the only sound seemed to be the slightly quickened breathing of Ted Jerningham, whose nerve was not quite as good as the others at affairs of this sort. Then came the sound of bolts being shot home, and footsteps coming into the office.

With a whispered "Stay there," Drummond glided across towards the door like a shadow, moving with uncanny silence for such a big man. And a moment or two afterwards someone came into the office. Jerningham, crouching against the crook behind the counter, could see the outline of a figure framed in the faint light that filtered in from a street lamp through the fanlight over the door. Then there was a click, and the electric light was switched on.

For a second the new-comer failed to see them; then, with a sudden gasp he stiffened, and stood staring at them rigidly. It was Cohen, the unpleasant little clerk, returning from an evening out, which accounted for the front door having been unbolted. And undoubtedly his luck was out. Because, having seen the two of them there behind the counter, he somewhat naturally failed to look for anybody else. It would not have made any great difference if he had, but the expression on his face as he felt two enormous hands close gently but firmly round his throat from behind caused even the phlegmatic Ginger to chuckle grimly.

"Out with the light," snapped Drummond, "then help me lash him up and gag him."

It was done quickly and deftly, and for the second time in a week the wretched Cohen was laid under his own counter to cool. It had been carried out as noiselessly as possible, but it was five minutes before Drummond again led the way cautiously up the stairs. And during that five minutes the three men listened with every sense alert, striving to differentiate between the ordinary street noises and anything unusual in the house above them. But not even Drummond's ears, trained as they had been for many nights in No Man's Land, could detect anything. All seemed as quiet as the grave.

"It probably is empty except for that little rat," he whispered to Jerningham. "But we'll take no chances."

In single file they crept up the stairs, Drummond leading. The door at the top was ajar, and for a while they stood in the carpeted passage above listening again.

"Along this passage are the clerks' offices," he explained in a low voice to the other two. "At the far end is another door which we shall probably find locked. Beyond that is the inner office, which we want."

"Well, let's get on wiv it, guv'nor," muttered Ginger Martin hoarsely. "There's no good in 'anging abaht."

Drummond switched on his electric torch, and flashed it cautiously round. Doors leading off the passage were open in most cases, and all the rooms were empty; it was obvious that none of the staff were about. And yet he felt an indefinable sense of danger, which he tried in vain to shake off. Somehow or other, he felt certain that they were not alone—that there were other people in the house, besides the trussed up clerk below. But Ginger Martin had no such presentiments, and was rapidly becoming impatient. To open the door at the end of the passage, if it should prove to be locked, was such child's play as to be absolutely contemptible. He wanted to get on with the safe, which might take time, instead of fooling round in a passage listening for mice.

At last Drummond moved slowly forward with the other two just behind him. Whatever he may have thought he had every intention of going through with the job, and delay in such cases only tends to turn vague fears into certain realities. Gently he tried the door at the end of the passage; as he had anticipated it was locked.

"'Old the light, guv'nor, so that it shines on the blinkin' key-'ole!" said Ginger Martin impatiently. "I'll get this open as easy as kiss yer 'and."

Without a sound, the cracksman set to work; his coarse features outlined in the circle of the torch, his ill-kept fingers handling his instruments as deftly as any surgeon. A little oil here and there; a steady pressure with a short pointed steel tool; a faint click.

"There you are, guv'nor," he muttered, straightening up. "Easy as kiss yer 'and. And if yer waits till I find me glove I'll open it for yer; but Ginger Martin's finger-prints are too well known to run any risks."

Still no sound came from anywhere, though the click as the lock shot back had seemed horribly loud in the silence. And then, just as Martin cautiously turned the handle and pushed open the door, Drummond stiffened suddenly and switched off his torch. He could have sworn that he heard the sound of voices close by.

Only for a second—they were instantly silenced; but just for that fraction of time as the door opened he felt certain he had heard men speaking.

"Wot's the matter?" he heard Martin's hoarse whisper come out of the darkness.

57

"Did you hear voices?" he breathed in reply. "I thought I did as you opened the door."

Once again the three men stood motionless, listening intently, but the sound was not repeated. Absolute silence reigned, broken only by the noise of their own breathing. And at last, after what seemed an interminable pause, Drummond switched on his torch again. The passage was empty; the door of the inner office was just in front of them. Almost he was persuaded that he must have made a mistake—that it had been his imagination. He peered through the keyhole: the room was in darkness. He turned the handle cautiously; the door gave to him; and still with his torch held well in front of him, he stepped into the room, turning the light into every corner. Not a trace of anyone; the inner office was absolutely empty. He flashed the light all round the walls, as far as he could see there was no other door—not even a window. Consequently the only way out was by the door through which they had just entered, which was obviously impossible for anyone to have done without his knowledge.

"It is all right!" he muttered, turning round to the other two. "Must have been my mistake. Let's get on with it."

"There's a mighty strong smell of cigar smoke," said Jerningham dubiously.

"No ventilation, old man," returned Drummond. "Hangs about for hours. No other door, no window. Now then, Ginger, let's tackle the big desk first. It looks pretty easy, even to me."

As he spoke he moved into the centre of the room, his torch lighting up the big roll-top desk.

"Right-ho, guv'nor. Keep the beam on the keyhole——"

The crook bent over his task, only to straighten up suddenly as all the lights went on.

"Yer damned fool!" he snarled. "Switch 'em off! It ain't safe."

"I didn't put 'em on!" snapped Drummond.

"Nor I," said Jerningham.

For a moment or two no one spoke; then Ginger Martin made a wild dive for the door. But the door which had opened so easily a few moments before now refused to budge, though he tugged at it, cursing horribly. And after a while he gave it up, and turned on Drummond like a wild beast.

"You've trapped me, yer —— swine. I'll get even with you over this if I swing for it!"

But Drummond, to whom the presence of actual danger was as meat and drink, took not the slightest notice. His brain, ice-cold and clear, was moving rapidly. It had not been a mistake, he had heard voices—voices which came from that very room in which they now were. Men had been there—men who had got out by some other way. And Ginger Martin was trapped—all of them. More out of thoughtlessness than anything else, he brushed the swearing crook aside with the back of his hand—much as one brushes away a troublesome fly.

And Martin, feeling as if he'd been kicked in the mouth by a horse, ceased to swear....

It was uncanny—devilish. The room empty, save for them, suddenly flooded with light. But by whom? Drummond felt they were being watched. But by whom? And then suddenly he heard Ted Jerningham's voice, low and tense.

"There's a man watching us, Hugh. I can see his eyes. In that big safe door."

Like a flash, Drummond swung round, and looked at the safe. Ted was right; he could see the eyes himself, and they were fixed on him with an expression of malignant fury through a kind of opening that looked like the slit in a letter box. For a moment or two they remained there, staring at him, then they disappeared, and the opening through which he had seen them disappeared also, and seemed to become part of the door. And it was just as he was moving towards this mysterious safe to examine it closer that with a sudden clang, another opening appeared—one much larger than the first. He stopped involuntarily as something was thrown through into the room—something which hissed and spluttered.

For a moment he gazed at it uncomprehendingly as it lay on the floor; then he gave a sudden, tense order.

"On your faces—for your lives!" His voice cut through the room like a knife. "Behind the desk, you fools! It's a bomb!"

8

In which the bag of nuts is found by accident

It was the desk that saved Drummond, and with him Ted Jerningham. Flat on their faces, their arms covering their heads, they lay on the floor waiting, as in days gone by they had waited for the bursting of a too-near crump. They heard Ginger Martin, as he blundered round the room, and then—suddenly it came.

There was a deafening roar, and a sheet of flame which seemed to fill the room. Great lumps of the ceiling rained down and the big roll top desk, cracked in pieces and splintered into matchwood, fell over on top of them. But it had done its work: it had borne the full force of the explosion in their direction. As a desk its day was past; it had become a series of holes roughly held together by fragments of wood.

So much Drummond could see by the aid of his torch. With the explosion all the lights had gone out, and for a while he lay pressed against Ted Jerningham trying to recover his wits. His head was singing like a bursting kettle: his back felt as if it was broken where a vast lump of ceiling had hit him. But after moving his legs cautiously and then his arms, he decided that he was still alive. And having arrived at that momentous conclusion the necessity for prompt action became evident. A bomb bursting in London is not exactly a private affair.

"Are you all right, Ted?" he muttered hoarsely, his mouth full of plaster and dust.

"I think so, old man," answered Jerningham, and Drummond heaved a sigh of relief. "I got a whack on the back of the head from something."

Drummond scrambled to his feet, and switched on his torch. The wreckage was complete, but it was for the third member of the party that he was looking. And after a moment or two he found him, and cursed with a vigorous fury that boded ill for the person who had thrown the bomb, if he ever met him.

For Ginger Martin, being either too frightened or too ignorant, had not done as he was told. There had been no desk between him and the bomb when it burst, and what was left of him adorned a corner. There was nothing to be done: the unfortunate crook would never again burgle a safe. And the only comfort to Drummond was that death must have been absolutely instantaneous.

"Poor devil," he muttered. "Someone is going to pay for this."

And then he felt Ted Jerningham clutching his arm.

"It's blown a hole in the wall, man. Look."

It was true: he could see the light of a street lamp shining through a great jagged hole.

"Some bomb," he muttered. "Let's clear."

He gave a final flash of his torch round the floor, as they moved towards the shattered wall, and then suddenly stopped.

"What's that?"

Right in the centre of the beam, lying in the middle of the floor, was a small chamois leather bag. It seemed unhurt, and, without thinking, Hugh picked it up and put it in his pocket. Then switching off the torch, they both clambered through the hole, dropped on to a lean-to roof, and reached the ground.

They were at the back of the house in some deserted mews, and rapidity of movement was clearly indicated. Already a crowd was hurrying to the scene of the explosion, and slipping quietly out of the dark alley, they joined in themselves.

"Go home, Ted," said Drummond. "I must get the others."

"Right, old man." He made no demur, but just vanished quietly, while his leader slouched on towards the front door of number 5, Green Street. The police were already beating on it, while a large knot of interested spectators giving gratuitous advice stood around them. And in the crowd Drummond could see six of his gang: six anxious men who had determined—police or no

60

police—to get upstairs and see what had happened. In one and all their minds was a sickening fear, that the man they followed had at last bitten off more than he could chew—that they'd find him blown to pieces in the mysterious room upstairs.

And then, quite clear and distinct above the excited comments of the crowd, came the hooting of an owl. A strange sound to hear in a London street, but no one paid any attention. Other more engrossing matters were on hand, more engrossing, that is, to all except the six men who instantaneously swung half round as they heard it. For just a second they had a glimpse of a huge figure standing in the light of a lamp-post on the other side of the street—then it disappeared; and with astonishing celerity they followed its example. Whoever had been hurt it was not Drummond; and that, at the moment, was all they were concerned with.

By devious routes they left the scene of the explosion—each with the same goal in his mind. The owl had only hooted once, which meant that they were to reassemble as soon as possible; the second call, which meant disperse, had not been given. And so within an hour six young men, shorn of all disguise and clad in immaculate evening clothes, were admitted to Drummond's house in Brook Street by a somewhat sleepy Denny.

They found Hugh arrayed in a gorgeous dressing-gown with a large tankard of beer beside him, and his wife sitting on the arm of his chair.

"Beer, souls," he grunted. "In the corner, as usual."

"What happened, old lad?" asked Peter Darrell.

"I got handed the frozen mitten. I asked for bread, and they put across a half-brick. To be absolutely accurate we got into the room all right, and having got in we found we couldn't get out. Then someone switched on the light, and bunged a bomb at us through a hole in the door. Quite O.K., old girl"—he put a reassuring arm round Phyllis's waist—"I think we'd be still there if they hadn't."

"Is Ted all right?" asked Toby Sinclair.

"Yes. Ted's all right. Got a young load of bricks in his back when the ceiling came down—but he's all right. It's the other poor devil—Ginger Martin." His face was grim and stern, and the others waited in silence for him to continue.

"There was a big desk in the room, and the bomb fell on one side of it. Ted and I gave our well-known impersonation of an earthworm on the other, which saved us. Unfortunately, Ginger Martin, elected to run round in small circles and curse. And he will curse no more."

"Dead?" Peter Darrell's voice was low.

"Very," answered Drummond quietly. "In fact, he's now giving his well-known impersonation of a wallpaper. The poor blighter was blown to pieces. If he'd done what I'd told him he wouldn't have been, but that's beside the point. He was working for me, and he was killed while he was doing so. And I don't like that happening."

"Oh! my dear," said Phyllis. "I do wish you'd give it up. You've escaped this time, but sooner or later they'll get you. It isn't worth it."

Drummond shook his head, and again encircled his wife's waist with his arm.

"You wouldn't like me to let that poor devil's death go unavenged, would you?" He looked up at her, and she shrugged her shoulders resignedly. A year of marriage with this vast husband of hers had convinced her of the futility of arguing with him once his mind was made up. "Not that the country will be appreciably worse off for his departure, but that's not the point. He was doing a job for me when it happened, and I don't stand for that at all."

"What do you propose to do?" demanded Jerry Seymour, thoughtfully refilling his glass.

"Well, there, old son, at the moment you have me beat," conceded Hugh. "I sort of figured it out this way. Whoever the bird is who bunged that bomb, he recognised me as being the leader of our little bunch. I mean it was me he was staring at through the door with eyes bubbling over with tenderness and love. It was me that bally bomb was intended for—not Ginger Martin, though he was actually doing the work. And if this cove is prepared to wreck his own office just to get me out of the way—I guess I must be somewhat unpopular."

"The reasoning seems extraordinarily profound," murmured Peter.

"Now the great point is—does he know who I am?" continued Hugh. "Is the little treasure now saying to himself, what time he lowers the evening cup of bread-and-milk, 'That has settled the hash of one Hugh Drummond,' or is he merely saying, 'I have nastily disintegrated the leader of the Black Gang'?"

"But what's it matter anyway?" demanded Toby. "He hasn't disintegrated you, and he's smashed up his own office—so I fail to see where he wins the grand piano."

"That, old Toby, is where you show yourself incapable of grasping the finer points of the situation." Hugh thoughtfully lit a cigarette. "Our great difficulty, before Zaboleff was kind enough to present us with the address of their headquarters, was to get in touch with the man at the top. And now the headquarters are no more. No man can work in an office with periodical boulders falling on his head from the roof, and a large hole in the wall just behind him. I mean there's no privacy about it. And so—unless he knows me—he won't be able to carry on the good work when he finds that neither of my boots has reached the top of St. Paul's. We shall be parted again—which is dreadful to think of. There's no cheery little meeting ground where we can foregather for the matutinal Martini or even Manhattan. Why, we might even pass one another in the street as complete strangers."

"I get you," said Peter. "And you don't know him."

"Not well enough to call him Bertie. There's a humpbacked blighter up there who calls himself a count, and on whom I focused the old optic for about two seconds the other evening. But whether he's the humorist who bunged the bomb or not is a different matter." He glanced up as the door opened. "What is it, Denny?"

"I found this bag, sir, in the pocket of the coat you were wearing to-night."

His servant came into the room carrying the chamois leather bag, which he handed to Drummond.

"Will you be wanting anything more to-night, sir?"

"No, thank you, Denny. You toddle off to bye-bye. And give Mrs. Denny a chaste salute from Mr. Darrell."

"Very good, sir!"

The door closed behind him, and Hugh stared thoughtfully at the bag in his hand.

"I'd forgotten about this. Saw it lying on the floor, just before we hopped it. Hullo! it's sealed."

"For goodness' sake be careful, boy!" cried Phyllis. "It may be another bomb."

Hugh laughed and ripped open the bag; then his eyes slowly widened in amazement as he saw the contents.

"Great Scott!" he cried. "What the devil have we got here?"

He emptied the bag out on to the table, and for a moment or two the others stared silently at half a dozen objects that flashed and glittered with a thousand fires. Five of them were white; but the sixth—appreciably larger than the others, and they were the size of walnuts—was a wonderful rose pink.

"What on earth are they? Lumps of glass?"

With a hand that shook a little, Toby Sinclair picked one of them up and examined it.

"No, you fellows," he muttered, "they're diamonds!"

"Rot!" cried Hugh incredulously.

"They're diamonds," repeated Toby. "I happen to know something about precious stones. These are diamonds."

"But they must be worth a lot," said Phyllis, picking up the pink one.

"Worth a lot," said Toby dazedly. "Worth a lot! Why, Mrs. Hugh, they are literally worth untold gold in the right market. They are absolutely priceless. I've never even thought of such stones. That one that you're holding in your hand would be worth over a quarter of a million pounds, if you could get the right buyer."

For a moment no one spoke; then Hugh laughed cheerily.

"Bang goes next month's dress allowance, old thing!" He swept them all into the bag, and stood up. "I'm laying even money that the bomb-thrower is coughing some and then again over his bread-and-milk. This bag must have been in the desk." His shoulders began to shake. "How frightfully funny!"

9

In which there is a stormy supper party at the Ritz

It was just about the time that Ginger Martin's wife became, all unconsciously, a widow, that the sitting-room bell of a certain private suite in the Ritz was rung. The occupants of the room were two in number—a man and a woman—and they had arrived only that morning from the Continent. The man, whose signature in the register announced him to be the Reverend Theodosius Longmoor—looked a splendid specimen of the right sort of clergyman. Tall, broad-shouldered, with a pair of shrewd, kindly eyes and a great mass of snow-white hair, he was the type of man who attracted attention wherever he went, and in whatever society he found himself. A faint twang in his speech betrayed his nationality, and, indeed, he made no secret of it. He was an American born and bred, who had been seeing first hand for himself some of the dreadful horrors of the famine which was ravaging Central Europe.

And with him had gone his daughter Janet—that faithful, constant companion of his, who since her mother's death had never left him. She was a good-looking girl, too—though perhaps unkind people might have said girlhood's happy days had receded somewhat into the past. Thirty, perhaps—even thirty-five—though her father always alluded to her as "My little girl."

There was something very sweet and touching about their relationship; his pride in her and her simple, loving admiration for Dad. Only that evening before dinner they had got into conversation in the lounge with a party of American globe-trotters, who had unanimously voted them quite charming.

"I feel," had said the Reverend Theodosius, "that it is almost wicked our staying in such an hotel as this, after the dreadful things we've seen. How my little girl stood it all I don't know." He took his daughter's hand and patted it lovingly.

"I guess," said Janet with her faint, sweet smile, "I guess the Dad deserves it. Why he nearly worked himself ill doing relief work and things out there in Vienna and places."

"Is there any lack of funds, Mr. Longmoor?" asked one lady. "One feels one ought to do something to help."

The Reverend Theodosius gave her one of his rare sweet smiles.

"There was when I left," he murmured. "You'd never believe how money goes out there, and really the poor children have very little to show for it."

"Too bad—too bad." A square-jawed man who was a member of the party beckoned to a passing waiter. "Say, Mr. Longmoor, will you drink a cocktail with me? And your daughter, too?"

64

"It is very good of you, sir," answered the clergyman, with a courteous bow. "My little girl has never even tasted one and I think perhaps she had better not. What do you think, my child?"

"I'd love to try, Daddy, dear," she said coaxingly. "Do you think I might? Or would it make my head go funny?"

They all laughed.

"That settles it, Miss Longmoor," cried the man. "I've ordered one for you, and if you don't drink it your father will have to drink two."

Undoubtedly a charming couple had been the verdict of these chance acquaintances—so simple, so fresh, so unassuming in these days of complexity and double-dealing. The only pity of it was, as the square-jawed man remarked to his wife at dinner, that the very quality of child-like simplicity which made them so charming was the one which laid them open to the most bare-faced swindling if they ever came up against blackguards.

After dinner they had all drunk coffee together, and then, because his little Janet was tired, the Reverend Theodosius and his daughter had retired after accepting an invitation to dinner the next day.

"Who are they?" asked Janet, as they entered their sitting room.

"That square-jawed man is John Pendel," answered her father, thoughtfully lighting a cigar. "Worth about three million. He's good for dining with, though I'm not over here on any side-shows."

And then for two hours until he got up and rang the bell, the Reverend Theodosius remained engrossed in work; while his little Janet, lying on the sofa, displayed considerably more leg than one would have expected a vicar's daughter even to possess. And occasional gurgles of laughter seemed to prove that Guy de Maupassant appeals to a more catholic audience than he would have suspected.

She was knitting decorously when the waiter came in, and her father ordered a little supper to be sent up.

"Some chicken, please, and a little foie gras. I am expecting a friend very soon—so lay for three. Some champagne—yes. Perrier Jouet '04 will do. I'm afraid I don't know much about wine. And a little Vichy water for my daughter."

The waiter withdrew, and the Reverend Theodosius chuckled.

"There's a very good bath you can empty it down, my dear," he said. "But I don't think my little Janet should drink champagne so late. It might make her head go funny."

She smiled and then grew serious.

"What time do you expect Zadowa?"

"He should have been here by now. I don't know why he's late."

"Did you see him this afternoon?"

"No. I was down at the office, but only for a short while."

The sound of voices outside the door caused Janet to resume her knitting, and the next moment Count Zadowa was announced. For an appreciable time after the waiter had withdrawn he stood staring at them: then a smile crossed his face.

"Magnificent," he murmured. "Superb. Madame, I felicitate you. Well though I know your powers, this time you have excelled yourself."

"Cut that out, and get to business," returned little Janet shortly, "I'm tired."

"But should we be interrupted," remarked the Reverend Theodosius, "we have just returned from an extensive tour in the famine-stricken area round Vienna."

The Count bowed and smiled again.

"*C'est entendu*," he said quietly. "And now we will certainly get to business. For I have the most wonderful news for you, *mes amis*."

A warning gesture from the girl announced the arrival of supper, and for a while the conversation turned on the rival merits of different types of soup kitchen. And it was not until the outer door finally closed behind the waiter, that the Reverend Theodosius bit the end off another cigar and stared at his visitor with eyes from which every trace of kindliness had vanished.

"It's about time you did have some good news, Zadowa," he snapped. "Anything more damned disgraceful than the way you've let this so-called Black Gang, do you in, I've never heard of."

But the other merely smiled quietly.

"I admit it," he murmured. "Up to date they have scored a faint measure of success—exaggerated, my friends, greatly exaggerated by the papers. To-night came the reckoning, which incidentally is the reason why I am a little late. To-night"—he leaned forward impressively—"the leader of the gang himself honoured me with a visit. And the leader will lead no more."

"You killed him," said the girl, helping herself to champagne.

"I did," answered the Count. "And without the leader I think we can ignore the gang."

"That's all right as far as it goes," said the Reverend Theodosius in a slightly mollified tone. "But have you covered all your traces? In this country the police get peevish over murder."

The Count gave a self-satisfied smile.

"Not only that," he remarked, "but I have made it appear as if he had killed himself. Listen, my friends, and I will give you a brief statement of the events of the past few days. It was the day before the affair at Sheffield which caused such a commotion in the papers that I suddenly found out that the leader of this gang had discovered my headquarters in Hoxton. I was actually talking to that wretched man Latter in my office at the time, when I heard outside the call of an owl. Now from information I had received, that was the rallying call of their gang, and I dashed into the passage. Sure enough, standing by the door at the end was a huge man covered from head to foot in black. Whether it was bravado that made him give the cry, or whether it was a ruse to enable him to see me, is immaterial now. As I say—he is dead. But—and this is the point—it made me decide that the office there, convenient though it was, would have to be given up. There were far too many incriminating documents to allow me to run the risk of a police raid; and since I frankly admit now that I was not at all sure what were the relations between this gang and the police, I decided to move my headquarters."

Count Zadowa helped himself to a sandwich before continuing, with a pleasant feeling that the motionless attention of the Reverend Theodosius was a compliment to his powers as a raconteur. And as the hunchback reflected complacently, there was no falling off in this story—no anti-climax.

"To-night," he continued, sipping his glass, "I was completing the final sorting out of my papers with my secretary, when the electric warning disc on my desk glowed red. Now the office was empty, and the red light meant that someone had opened the door outside. I heard nothing, which only made it all the more suspicious. So between us we gathered up every important paper, switched off all lights, and went out through the secret door. Then we waited."

He turned to the clergyman, still motionless save for a ceaseless tapping of his left knee with his hand.

"As you know, monsieur," he proceeded, "there is an opening in that door through which one can see into the room. And through that opening I watched developments. After a while a torch was switched on at the further door, and I heard voices. And then the man holding the torch came cautiously in. He was turning it into every corner, but finally he focused it on the desk. I heard him speak to one of his companions, who came into the beam of light and, started to pick the lock. And it was then that I switched on every light, and closed the other door electrically. They were caught—caught like rats in a trap."

The hunchback paused dramatically, and drained his champagne. If he was expecting any laudatory remarks on the part of his audience he was disappointed. But the Reverend Theodosius and his little Janet might have been carved out of marble, save for that ceaseless tapping by the man of his left knee. In fact, had Count Zadowa been less pleased with himself and less sure of the effect he was about to cause he might have had a premonition of coming danger. There was something almost terrifying in the big clergyman's immobility.

"Like rats in a trap," repeated the hunchback gloatingly. "Two men I didn't know, and—well, you know who the other was. True he had his mask on by way of disguise, but I recognized him at once. That huge figure couldn't be mistaken—it was the leader of the Black Gang himself."

"And what did you do, Zadowa?"

The Reverend Theodosius's voice was very soft.

"How did you dispose of one or all those men so that no suspicion is likely to rest on you?"

The hunchback rubbed his hands together gleefully.

"By an act which, I think you will agree, is very nearly worthy of yourself, *monsieur*. To shoot was impossible—because I am not sufficiently expert with a revolver to be sure of killing them. No—nothing so ordinary as that. They saw me watching them: 'I can see his eyes, Hugh,' said one of them to the leader, and I remember suddenly that in the passage not far from where I stood were half a dozen bombs—— What is it, *monsieur*?"

He paused in alarm at the look on the clergyman's face as he slowly rose.

"Bombs!" he snarled. "Bombs! Tell me what you did, you dreg!"

"Why," stammered the frightened hunchback "I threw one into the room. I no longer wanted it as an office, and ... Ah, heaven, don't murder me! ... What have I done?"

His words died away in a dreadful gurgle, as the clergyman, his face diabolical with fury, sprang on him and gripped him by the throat. He shook the hunchback as a terrier shakes a rat, cursing horribly under his breath—and for a moment or two it seemed as if the other's fear was justified. There was murder in the big man's face, until the touch of the girl's hand on his arm steadied him and brought him to his senses. With a last spasm of fury he hurled the wretched Zadowa into a corner, and left him lying there; then his iron self-control came back to him.

"Get up," he ordered tensely, "and answer some questions."

Trembling all over, the hunchback staggered to his feet and came into the centre of the room.

"*Monsieur*," he whined, "I do not understand. What have I done?"

"You don't need to understand!" snarled the clergyman. "Tell me exactly what happened when the bomb burst."

"It killed the three men, *monsieur*," stammered the other.

"Curse the three men!" He lifted his clenched fist, and Zadowa shrank back. "What happened to the room?"

"It was wrecked utterly. A great hole was blown in the wall."

"And what happened to the desk?"

"I don't know exactly, *monsieur*," stammered the other. "I didn't go back to see. But it must have been blown to matchwood. Only as there was nothing inside of importance it makes no odds."

"Did you look in the secret drawer at the back of the centre opening? You didn't know there was one, did you? Only I knew of its existence, and short of taking the desk to pieces no one would be able to find it. And you took the desk to pieces, Zadowa, didn't you? You blew it to pieces, Zadowa, didn't you? Just to kill the leader of this trumpery gang, Zadowa, you cursed fool!"

Step by step, the hunchback was retreating before the other, terror convulsing his face, until the wall brought him to an abrupt stop.

"You blew the desk to pieces, Zadowa," continued the Reverend Theodosius, standing in front of him, "a desk that contained the six most perfect diamonds in the world, Zadowa. With your wretched bomb, you worm, you destroyed a fortune. What have you got to say?"

"I didn't know, *monsieur*," cringed the other. "How could I know? When were they put there?"

"I put them there this afternoon for safety. Not in my wildest imagination did I dream that you would start throwing bombs about the place."

"Perhaps they are not destroyed," stammered the hunchback hopefully.

"In which case they are now in the hands of the police. You have one chance, Zadowa, and only one. It is that those diamonds are in the hands of the police. If they are and you can get them—I will say no more."

"But if they have been destroyed, *monsieur*?" muttered the other.

"Then, Zadowa, I am afraid you will share their fate."

Almost indifferently the clergyman turned back into the room, taking no notice whatever of the wretched man who followed him on his knees begging for mercy. And then after a while the hunchback pulled himself together and stood up.

"It was a mistake, *monsieur*," he said quietly, "which I deeply regret. It was, however, you must admit, hardly my fault. I will do my best."

"Let us hope, then, for your sake, Zadowa, that your best will be successful. Now go."

He pointed to the door, and without another word the hunchback went.

"I am glad you were here to-night, my dear," remarked the Reverend Theodosius. "I don't often lose my temper, but I very nearly killed that man this evening." The girl rose and came over to where he was standing.

"I don't understand, *mon chére*," she said quietly. "What diamonds are these you talk of?"

The man gave a short, hard laugh.

"I didn't tell you," he answered. "There was no object in your knowing for a time. I know your weakness where jewels are concerned too well, my dear; I got them the night before last in Amsterdam. Do you remember that Russian—Stanovitch? That wasn't his real name. He was the eldest son of the Grand Duke Georgius, and he had just arrived from Russia."

"The man who took that overdose of his sleeping-draught?" whispered the girl barely above her breath.

The Reverend Theodosius smiled grimly.

"So they decided," he remarked. "He confided in me the night before he came to his sad end what he had been doing in Russia. His father had hidden the family heirlooms from the Bolshevists, and our young friend went over to retrieve them. Most ingenious—the way he got them out of Russia. Such a pity he had a lapse with his sleep dope."

And now the Reverend Theodosius was snarling like a mad dog.

"By heavens, girl—do you wonder that I nearly killed that fool Zadowa? The *coup* of a lifetime—safely brought off. Not a trace of suspicion on me—not a trace. I know I said I wasn't over here on sideshows, but I couldn't have been expected to let such a chance slip by. And then, after having got them safely into this country to lose them like that. Why, do you know that one of them was the rose diamond of the Russian Crown jewels?"

The girl's eyes glistened, then she shrugged her shoulders.

"They would have been unsaleable, *mon ami*," she said quietly.

"Don't you believe it," snapped the other. "There are markets for anything in this world, if one takes the trouble to look for them."

He was pacing up and down the room, and for a while she stood watching him in silence.

"I'm glad I didn't know about them till now," she said at length. "I might not have stopped you killing him, if I had. And it would have been rather awkward."

He gave a short laugh, and threw the end of his cigar into the grate.

"No good crying over spilt milk, my dear. Let's go to bed."

But little Janet still stood by the table watching him thoughtfully.

"What are you thinking about?"

"I was thinking about a rather peculiar coincidence," she answered quietly. "You were too worried over the diamonds to notice it—but it struck me instantly. The leader of this gang—this huge man whom Zadowa killed to-night. Did you notice what his Christian name was?"

The Reverend Theodosius shook his head.

"It was Hugh—Zadowa heard one of the others call him by name. Hugh, *mon ami*; Hugh—and a huge man. A coincidence, I think."

The man gave a short laugh.

"A very long one, my dear. Too long to bother about."

"It would be a pity if he was dead," she went on thoughtfully. "I would have liked to see my Hugh Drummond again."

"If he has been killed, if your supposition is correct," returned the man, "it will do something towards reconciling me to the loss of the diamonds. But I don't think it's likely. And incidentally he is the only side-show I am going to allow myself during this trip."

Little Janet laughed softly.

"I wonder," she said, "I wonder. Let us, as you say, go to bed."

10

In which Hugh Drummond
makes a discovery

The prospect in front of Count Zadowa, *alias* Mr. Atkinson, was not a very alluring one, and the more he thought about it the less he liked it. Either the diamonds were blown to dust, or they were in the hands of the authorities. In the first event he had the Reverend Theodosius to reckon with; in the second the police. And for preference the police won in a canter.

He was under no delusions was the hunchback. This mysterious man who signed all his communications by the enigmatic letter X, and whose real appearance was known probably only to the girl who was his constant companion, so wonderful and varied were his disguises, was not a person whom it paid to have any delusions about. He paid magnificently, even lavishly, for work well done: for failure he took no excuse. Even long association did not mitigate the offence. With a shudder Count Zadowa remembered the fate of certain men he had known in the past, men who had been employed, even as he was now employed, on one of the innumerable schemes of their chief. No project, from the restoration of a monarchy to the downfall of a business combine, was too great for the man who now called himself the Reverend Theodosius Longmoor. All that mattered was that there should be money in it. Why he should be interesting himself in the spread of Communism in England it was not for Count Zadowa to inquire, even though he was the head of that particular activity. Presumably he was being paid for it by others; it was no business of Count Zadowa's.

And as he undressed that night in the quiet hotel in Bloomsbury, where he lived, the hunchback cursed bitterly under his breath. It was such a cruel stroke of luck. How much he had dreaded that first interview with his chief he had hardly admitted even to himself. And then had come the heaven-sent opportunity of killing the leader of the Black Gang in perfect safety; of making it appear that the three men inside the room, and who had no business to be inside the room, had blown themselves up by mistake. How was he to know about the diamonds: how could he possibly be expected to know? And once again he cursed, while the sweat glistened on his forehead as he realized his predicament.

He had already decided that his only method lay in going down to the office next morning as usual. He would find it, of course, in the possession of the police, and would be told what had happened. And then he would have to trust to luck to discover what he could. Perhaps—and at the thought of it he almost started to dress again—perhaps the desk was not utterly ruined. Perhaps the diamonds were there, even now, in the secret drawer. And then he realised that if he went to his office at two o'clock in the morning, it must look suspicious. No; waiting was the only possibility, and Count Zadowa waited. He even went so far as to get into bed, but Count Zadowa did not sleep.

Punctually at half-past nine the next morning he arrived at 5, Green Street. As he had expected, a constable was standing at the door.

"Who are you, sir?" The policeman was barring his entrance.

"My name is Atkinson," said the Count, with well-feigned surprise. "May I ask what you're doing here?"

"Haven't you heard, sir?" said the constable. "There was a bomb outrage here last night. In your office upstairs."

"A bomb outrage?" Mr. Atkinson gazed at the constable in amazement, and a loafer standing by began to laugh.

"Not 'arf, guv'nor," he remarked cheerfully. "The 'ole ruddy place is gone to blazes."

"You dry up," admonished the policeman. "Move along, can't you?"

"Orl rite, orl rite," grumbled the other, shambling off. "Not allowed to live soon, we won't be."

"You'd better go up, sir," continued the constable. "The Inspector is upstairs."

Mr. Atkinson needed no second invitation. Taking no notice of the half-dozen clerks who had gathered in a little group discussing the affair, he passed along the passage into his own room. And the scene that met his eyes reflected credit on the manufacturer of the bomb. Viewed by the light of day which came streaming in through the great hole in the wall the ruin was complete. In the centre—and it was there Mr. Atkinson's eyes strayed continuously even while he was acknowledging the greetings of the Inspector—stood the remnants of the desk. And as he looked at it any faint hope he may have cherished vanished completely. It was literally split to pieces in every direction; there was not left a hiding-place for a pea, much less a bag of diamonds.

"Not much in the office, sir, which was lucky for you."

The Inspector was speaking and Mr. Atkinson pulled himself together. He had a part to play, and whatever happened no suspicions must be aroused.

"I feel quite staggered, Inspector." His glance travelled to a sinister-looking heap in the corner—a heap roughly covered with an old rug. The wall above it was stained a dull red, and from under the rug stretched out two long streams of the same colour—streams which were not yet dry.

"What on earth has happened?"

"There seems very little doubt about that, sir," remarked the Inspector. "I have reconstructed the whole thing with the help of your clerk here, Mr. Cohen. It appears that last night about twelve o'clock three men entered your office downstairs. They bound and gagged Cohen—and then they came on up here. Evidently their idea was burglary. What happened, then, of course, it is hard to say exactly. Presumably they started using explosive to force your safe, and explosive is funny stuff even for the expert."

The Inspector waved a hand at the heap in the corner.

"And he—poor devil, was quite an expert in his way. One of the three men, Mr. Atkinson—or what's left of him, Ginger Martin—an old friend of mine."

For a moment Mr. Atkinson's heart stood still. One of the three men! Then, where in Heaven's name, were the other two?

"One of the three, Inspector," he said at length, steadying himself. "But what happened to the others?"

"That is the amazing thing, sir," answered the Inspector. "I can but think that though three men entered the office downstairs, only Martin can have been in here at the time of the explosion." He pulled back the blood-stained rug, and with a shudder Mr. Atkinson contemplated what was underneath. He recognized the face; sure enough it was the man who had run round the room when he found himself trapped. But there was no trace of anyone else. The mangled remnants had formed one man and one man only. Then what, he reflected again,—what had become of the other two? He knew they had been in there at the time of the explosion, and as he vaguely listened to the Inspector's voice his mind was busy with this new development.

They had been in there—the leader of the Black Gang and one of his pals. There was no trace of them now. Wherefore, somehow, by some miraculous means they must have escaped, and the soul of Count Zadowa grew sick within him. Not only had the whole thing been useless and unnecessary; not only had he incurred the wrath of his own leader, and unwelcome attention from the police, but, in addition, this mysterious being whom he had thought to kill was not dead but very much alive. He had two people up against him now, and he wasn't quite sure which of the two he feared most.

Suddenly he became aware that the Inspector was asking him a question.

"Why, yes," he said, pulling himself together, "that is so. I was leaving this office here, and had removed almost everything of value. Only some diamonds were left, Inspector—and they were in that desk. I have somewhat extensive dealings in precious stones. Was there any trace of them found?"

The Inspector laughed grimly.

"You see the room for yourself, sir. But that perhaps supplies us with the motive for the crime. I am afraid your diamonds are either blown to pieces, or in the hands of the other two men, whom I have every hope of laying my hands on shortly. There is no trace of them here."

In the hands of the other two men! The idea was a new one, which had not yet come into his calculations, so convinced had he been that all three men were dead. And suddenly he felt a sort of blinding certainty that the Inspector—though in ignorance of the real facts of the case—was right in his surmise. Diamonds are not blown to pieces by an explosion; scattered they might be—disintegrated, no. He felt he must get away to consider this new development. Where did he stand if the diamonds were indeed in the possession of the Black Gang? Would it help him or would it not, with regard to that implacable man at the Ritz?

He crossed over to the jagged hole in the wall and looked out.

"This has rather upset me, Inspector," he said, after a while. "The South Surrey Hotel in Bloomsbury will always find me."

"Right, sir!" The Inspector made a note, and then leaned out through the hole with a frown. "Get out of this, you there! Go on, or I'll have you locked up as a vagrant!"

"Orl rite, orl rite! Can't a bloke 'ave a bit o' fun when 'e ain't doing no 'arm?"

The loafer, who had been ignominiously moved on from the front door, scrambled down from the lean-to roof behind, and slouched away, muttering darkly. And he was still muttering to himself as he opened the door of a taxi a few minutes later, into which Mr. Atkinson hurriedly stepped. For a moment or two he stood on the pavement until it had disappeared from view; then his prowling propensities seemed to disappear as if by magic. Still with the same shambling gait, but apparently now with some definite object in his mind, he disappeared down a side street, finally coming to a halt before a public telephone-box. He gave one rapid look round, then he stepped inside.

"Mayfair 1234." He waited beating a tattoo with his pennies on the box. Things had gone well that morning—very well.

"Hullo, is that you, Hugh? Yes, Peter speaking. The man Atkinson is the hunchback. Stopping South Surrey Hotel, Bloomsbury. He's just got into a taxi and gone off to the Ritz. He seemed peeved to me.... Yes, he inquired lovingly about the whatnots.... What's that? You'll toddle round to the Ritz yourself. Right ho! I'll come, too. Cocktail time. Give you full details then."

The loafer stepped out of the box and shut the door. Then, still sucking a filthy clay pipe, he shambled off in the direction of the nearest Tube station. A slight change of attire before lining up at the Ritz seemed indicated.

And it would, indeed, have been a shrewd observer who would have identified the immaculately-dressed young gentleman who strolled into the Ritz shortly before twelve o'clock with the dissolute-looking object who had so aroused the wrath of the police a few hours previously in Hoxton. The first person he saw sprawling contentedly in an easy chair was Hugh Drummond, who waved his stick in greeting.

"Draw up Peter, old lad," he boomed, "and put your nose inside a wet."

Peter Darrell took the next chair, and his eyes glanced quickly round the lounge.

"Have you seen him, Hugh?" he said, lowering his voice. "I don't see anything answering to the bird growing about the place here."

"No," answered Hugh. "But from discreet inquiries made from old pimply-face yonder I find that he arrived here about ten o'clock. He was at once shown up to the rooms of a gent calling himself the Reverend Theodosius Longmoor, where, as far as I can make out, he has remained ever since. Anyway, I haven't seen him trotting up and down the hall, calling to his young; nor have either of the beadles at the door reported his departure. So here I remain like a bird in the wilderness until the blighter and his padre pal break covert. I want to see the Reverend Theodosius Longmoor, Peter."

A ball of wool rolled to his feet, and Hugh stooped to pick it up. The owner was a girl sitting close by, busily engaged in knitting some obscure garment, and Hugh handed her the wool with a bow.

"Thank you so much!" she said, with a pleasant smile. "I'm afraid I'm always dropping my wool all over the place."

"Don't mention it," remarked Hugh politely. "Deuced agile little thing—a ball of wool. Spend my life picking up my wife's. Everybody seems to be knitting these jumper effects now."

"Oh, this isn't a jumper," answered the girl a little sadly. "I've no time for such frivolities as that. You see, I've just come back from the famine stricken parts of Austria—and not only are the poor things hungry, but they can't get proper clothes. So just a few of us are knitting things for them—stock sizes, you know—big, medium, and small."

"How fearfully jolly of you!" said Hugh admiringly. "Dashed sporting thing to do. Awful affair, though, when the small size shrinks in the wash. The proud proprietor will burst out in all directions. Most disconcerting for all concerned."

The girl blushed faintly and Hugh subsided abashed in his chair.

"I must tell my wife about it," he murmured in confusion. "She's coming here to lunch, and she ought to turn 'em out like bullets from a machine gun—what?"

The girl smiled faintly as she rose.

"It would be very good of her if she would help," she remarked gently, and then, with a slight bow, she walked away in the direction of the lift.

"You know, old son," remarked Hugh, as he watched her disappearing, "it's an amazing affair when you really come to think of it. There's that girl with a face far superior to a patched boot and positively oozing virtue from every pore. And yet, would you leave your happy home for her? Look at her skirts—five inches too long; and yet she'd make a man an excellent wife. A heart of gold probably, hidden beneath innumerable strata of multi-coloured wools."

Completely exhausted he drained his cocktail, and leaned back in his chair, while Peter digested the profound utterance in silence. A slight feeling of lassitude was beginning to weigh on him owing to the atrocious hour at which he had been compelled to rise, and he felt quite unable to contribute any suitable addition to the conversation. Not that it was required: the ferocious frown on Drummond's face indicated that he was in the throes of thought and might be expected to give tongue in the near future.

"I ought to have a bit of paper to write it all down on, Peter," he remarked at length. "I was getting it fairly clear when that sweet maiden put me completely in the soup again. In fact, I was just going to run over the whole affair with you when I had to start chasing wool all over London. Where are we, Peter? That is the question. Point one: we have the diamonds—more by luck than good management. Point two: the hunchback gentleman who has a sufficiently strong constitution to live at the South Surrey Hotel in Bloomsbury has not got the diamonds. Point three: he, at the present moment is closeted with the Reverend Theodosius Longmoor upstairs. Point four: we are about to consume another cocktail downstairs. Well—bearing that little lot in mind, what happens when we all meet?"

"Yes, what!" said Peter, coming out of a short sleep.

"A policy of masterly inactivity seems indicated," continued Hugh thoughtfully. "We may even have to see them eat. But I can't buttonhole Snooks, or whatever the blighter's name is, and ask him if he bunged a bomb at me last night, can I? It would be so deuced awkward if he hadn't. As I said before, a brief survey of the devil-dodger's face might help. And, on the other hand, it might not. In fact, it is all very obscure, Peter—very obscure."

A slight snore was his only answer, and Hugh continued to ponder on the obscurity of the situation in silence. That several rays of light might have been thrown on it by a conversation then proceeding upstairs was of no help to him: nor could he have been expected to know that the fog of war was about to lift in a most unpleasantly drastic manner.

"Coincidence? Bosh!" the girl with the heart of gold was remarking at that very moment. "It's a certainty. Whether he's got the diamonds or not I can't say, but your big friend of last night, Zadowa, is sitting downstairs now drinking a cocktail in the lounge.

"And your big friend of last night is a gentleman with whom he and I"—she smiled thoughtfully at the Reverend Theodosius—"have a little account to settle."

"My account is not a little one," said the hunchback viciously.

"Amazing though it is, it certainly looks as if you were right, my dear," answered her father thoughtfully.

"Of course I'm right!" cried the girl. "Why, the darned thing is sticking out and barking at you. A big man, Christian name Hugh, was in Zadowa's office last night. Hugh Drummond is downstairs at the moment, having actually tracked Zadowa here. Of course, they're the same; an infant in arms could see it."

"Granted you're right," said the Reverend Theodosius, "I confess at the moment that I am a little doubtful as to how to turn the fact to our advantage. The fact is an interesting one, my dear, more than interesting; but it don't seem to me to come within the range of practical politics just at present."

"I wonder," said the girl. "His wife is coming here to lunch. You remember her—that silly little fool Phyllis Benton? And they live in Brook Street. It might be worth trying. If by any chance he has got the diamonds—well, she'll be very useful. And if he hasn't," she shrugged her shoulders, "we can easily return her if we don't want her."

The Reverend Theodosius smiled. Long-winded explanations between the two of them were seldom necessary. Then he looked at his watch.

"Short notice," he remarked; "but we'll try. No harm done if we fail."

He stepped over to the telephone, and put through a call. And having given two or three curt orders he came slowly back into the room.

"Chances of success very small, I'm afraid; but as you say, my dear, worth trying. And now I think I'll renew my acquaintance with Drummond. It would be wiser if you had lunch sent up here, Janet; just for the time our friend had better not connect us together in any way. And as for you, Zadowa"—his tone became curt—"you can go. Let us hope for your sake that Drummond has really got them."

"There's only one point," put in the girl; "his departure will be reported at once to Drummond. He's tipped both the men at the doors."

"Then in that case you'd better stop here," said the Reverend Theodosius. "I shall probably come up to lunch, but I might have it in the restaurant. I might"—he paused by the door—"I might even have it with Drummond and his friend."

With a short chuckle he left the room, and a minute or two later a benevolent clergyman, reading the *Church Times*, was sitting in the lounge just opposite Hugh and Peter. Through half-closed eyes Hugh took stock of him, wondering casually if this was the Reverend Theodosius Longmoor. If so, assuredly nothing more benevolent in the line of sky-pilots could well be imagined. And when a few minutes later the clergyman took a cigarette out of his case, and then commenced to fumble in his pockets for matches which he had evidently forgotten, Hugh rose and offered him one.

"Allow me, sir," he murmured, holding it out.

"I thank you, sir," said the clergyman, with a charming smile. "I'm so terribly forgetful over matches. As a matter of fact I don't generally smoke before lunch, but I've had such a distressing morning that I felt I must have a cigarette just to soothe my nerves."

"By Jove! that's bad," remarked Hugh. "Bath water cold, and all that?"

"Nothing so trivial, I fear," said the other. "No; a poor man who has been with me since ten has just suffered the most terrible blow. I could hardly have believed it possible here in London, but the whole of his business premises were wrecked by a bomb last night."

"You don't say so," murmured Hugh, sinking into a chair, and at the table opposite Peter Darrell opened one eye.

"All his papers—everything—gone. And it has hit me, too. Quite a respectable little sum of money—over a hundred pounds, gathered together for the restoration of the old oak chancel in my church—blown to pieces by this unknown miscreant. It's hard, sir, it's hard. But this poor fellow's loss is greater than mine, so I must not complain. To the best of my poor ability I have been helping him to bear his misfortune with fortitude and strength."

The clergyman took off his spectacles and wiped them, and Drummond stole a lightning glance at Darrell. The faintest shrug of his shoulders indicated that the latter had heard, and was as much in the dark as Hugh. That this was the Reverend Theodosius Longmoor was now obvious, but what a charming, courteous old gentleman! It seemed impossible to associate guilt with such a delightful person, and, if so, they had made a bad mistake. It was not the hunchback who had thrown the bomb; they were up another blind alley.

For a while Hugh chatted with him about the outrage, then he glanced at his watch.

"Nearly time for lunch, I think," said the clergyman. "Perhaps you would give a lonely old man the pleasure of your company."

"Very nice of you, but I'm expecting my wife," said Hugh. "She said she'd be here at one, and now it's a quarter past. Perhaps you'll lunch with us?"

"Charmed," said the clergyman, taking a note which a page-boy was handing to him on a tray. "Charmed." He glanced through the note, and placed it in his pocket. "The ladies, bless them! so often keep us waiting."

"I'll just go and ring up," said Drummond. "She may have changed her mind."

"Another prerogative of their sex," beamed his companion, as Drummond left him. He polished his spectacles and once more resumed his perusal of the *Church Times*, bowing in old-world fashion to two or three acquaintances who passed. And more and more was Peter Darrell becoming convinced that a big mistake had been made somewhere, when Hugh returned looking a little worried.

"Can't make it out, Peter," he said anxiously. "Just got through to Denny, and Phyllis left half an hour ago to come here."

"Probably doing a bit of shopping, old man," answered Peter reassuringly. "I say, Hugh, we've bloomered over this show."

Hugh glanced across the table where the clergyman was sitting, and suddenly Peter found his arm gripped with a force that made him cry out. He glanced at Hugh, and that worthy was staring at the clergyman with a look of speechless amazement on his face. Then he swung round, and his eyes were blazing.

"Peter!" he said tersely. "Look at him. The one trick that gives him away every time! Bloomered, have we? Great heavens above, man, it's Carl Peterson!"

A little dazedly Darrell glanced at the clergyman. He was still reading the *Church Times*, but with his left hand he was drumming a ceaseless tattoo on his knee.

11

In which Hugh Drummond and the Reverend Theodosius Longmoor take lunch together

"Rot, Hugh!" Peter turned a little irritably from his covert inspection of the Reverend Theodosius Longmoor. "You've got Peterson on the brain. Why, that old bird is no more like him than my boot."

"Nevertheless, it's Peterson," answered Drummond doggedly. "Don't look at him, Peter; don't let him think we're talking about him on any account. I admit he bears not the slightest resemblance to our one and only Carl, but he's no more unlike him than the Comte de Guy was that time in Paris. It's just that one little trick he can never shake off—that tapping with his left hand on his knee—that made me spot him."

"Well, granted you're right," conceded Darrell grudgingly, "what do we do now, sergeant-major?"

Drummond lit a cigarette thoughtfully before he replied. Half-hidden by a large luncheon party which was just preparing to move into the restaurant, he stole another look at the object of their remarks. With an expression of intense benevolence the Reverend Theodosius was chatting with an elderly lady, and on Drummond's face, as he turned back was a faint grin of admiration. Truly in the matter of disguises the man was a living marvel.

"I don't know, Peter," he answered after a while. "I've got to think this out. It's been so sudden that it's got me guessing. I know it's what we've been hoping for; it's what we wrote that letter to the paper for—to draw the badger. And by the Lord! we've drawn him, and the badger is Peterson. But somehow or other I didn't expect to find him disguised as a Mormon missionary residing at the Ritz."

"You're perfectly certain, Hugh?" said Peter, who was still far from convinced.

"Absolutely, old man," answered Drummond gravely. "The clergyman over there is Carl Peterson, late of the Elms, Godalming. And the game has begun again."

Darrell gave a short laugh as he noted the gleam in his leader's eyes.

"I'm thinking," he remarked soberly, "that this time the game is going to make us go all out."

"So much the better," grinned Hugh. "We'll add him to our collection, Peter, and then we'll present the whole damned bunch to the Zoo. And, in the meantime, he shall lunch with us when Phyllis arrives and prattle on theology to an appreciative audience. Incidentally it will appeal to his sense of humour; there's no difficulty about recognizing us."

"Yes," agreed Peter, "we start one up there. He doesn't know that we've spotted him. I wonder where the diamonds come in, Hugh?"

"Darned intimately, from what I know of the gentleman. But that's only one of several little points that require clearing up. And in the next few days, Peter, my boy—we will clear them up."

"Or be cleared up ourselves," laughed Darrell. "Look out, he's coming over."

They turned as the clergyman crossed the lounge towards them.

"Jolly old tum-tum beginning to shout for nourishment," said Hugh with an affable smile as he joined them. "My wife should be here at any moment now, Mr.—er——"

"Longmoor is my name," said the clergyman, beaming on them. "It is very charming of you to take such compassion on a lonely old man."

"Staying here all by yourself?" asked Drummond politely.

"No; my daughter is with me. The dear child has been my constant companion ever since my beloved wife's death some years ago."

He polished his glasses, which had become a little misty, and Drummond made noises indicative of sympathy.

"You wouldn't believe the comfort she has been to me. In these days, when it seems to me that the modern girl thinks of nothing but dancing and frivolity, it is indeed a blessing to find one who, while preserving her winsome sense of humour, devotes her life to the things that really matter. In our recent tour in Austria—I beg your pardon, you said———"

"Nothing," answered Drummond quietly. "You have been to Austria, you say?"

"Yes; we have just returned from a visit to the famine-stricken area," replied the clergyman. "Most interesting—but most terribly sad. You know—I don't think I caught your name."

"Drummond, Captain Drummond," answered Hugh mechanically. "And this is Mr. Darrell. I think I have had the pleasure of making your daughter's acquaintance already. She was manufacturing woollen garments for the Austrians down here, and I retrieved an elusive ball of wool for her."

"That is just my daughter all over, Captain Drummond," beamed the Reverend Theodosius. "Never wasting her time, always doing something for the good of humanity."

But at the moment it is to be regretted that Hugh was not worrying his head over the good of humanity. Inconceivable though it was, judged on the mere matter of appearance, that the Reverend Theodosius was Carl Peterson, it was still more inconceivable that the wool knitter with the heart of gold could be Irma. Of course Peterson might have changed his daughter—but if he hadn't, what then? What had he said to Peter Darrell when the girl, recognizing him all the time, was sitting in the next chair? How much had she overheard? And suddenly Hugh began to feel that he was floundering in deep waters. How many cards did the other side hold? And, what was even more important, how many of his own cards had they placed correctly? And glancing up he found the reverend gentleman's blue eyes fixed on him and glinting with a certain quizzical humour. Assuredly, reflected Drummond, it was up to him to find out, and that as soon as possible, exactly how matters stood. The trouble was how to set about it. To greet the Reverend Theodosius as a long-lost friend and ask him whether the disguise was donned to amuse the children would certainly precipitate affairs, but it would also throw one of his best cards on the table. And Carl Peterson was not a gentleman with whom it was advisable to weaken one's hand unnecessarily. So it all boiled down to a policy of waiting for the other side to play first, which, in view of the fact that he was getting distinctly peckish, seemed to Hugh to be an eminently sound decision.

He glanced at his watch and turned to Darrell.

"Confound the girl, Peter! She's nearly forty minutes late."

"Picked up a pal, old boy," answered that worthy. "Picked up a pal and they're masticating a Bath bun somewhere. Why not leave a message at the door, and let's get on with it? I'm darned hungry."

The Reverend Theodosius beamed from behind his spectacles.

"'Tis ever the same," he murmured gently. "But it is the prerogative of their sex."

"Well, let's toddle in and take nourishment," said Hugh, taking hold of the clergyman's arm with his hand and pushing him towards the restaurant. "Jove! Mr. Longmoor—you've got some pretty useful biceps on you."

The other smiled as if pleased with the compliment.

"Nothing to you, Captain Drummond, to judge by your size, but I think I may say I'm a match for most men. My ministry has led me into some very rough corners, and I have often found that where gentle persuasion fails, force will succeed."

"Quite so," murmured Drummond, gazing at the menu. "Nothing like a good one straight on the point of the jaw for producing a devout manner of living in the recipient. Often found that out myself. By the way, what about the daughter? Isn't she going to honour us?"

"Not to-day," answered the Reverend Theodosius. "She is lunching upstairs with the poor fellow I told you about, whose office was wrecked last night. He is sadly in need of comfort."

"I'll bet he is," agreed Hugh. "But if he put on one of those jolly little things she's knitting and trotted up and down Piccadilly he'd soon get all the money back for your chancel steps. The man I'm sorry for is the poor devil who was found adhering to the wall."

The Reverend Theodosius glanced at him thoughtfully, and Drummond realized he had made a slip.

"You seem to know quite a lot about it, Captain Drummond," murmured the other, dissecting a sardine.

"It's in the early editions of the evening papers," returned Hugh calmly. "Pictures and everything. The only thing they've left out is that reference to your little lump of dough."

"In such a dreadful thing as this, a trifle like that might well be overlooked," said the Reverend Theodosius. "But I understand from my poor friend upstairs that the police are satisfied that three scoundrels were involved in the crime. And two of them have escaped."

"Dirty dogs," said Hugh, frowning. "Now if all three had been found adhering to the furniture it might have reconciled you to the loss of those hundred acid drops."

"In fact," continued the clergyman, helping himself to some fish, "the whole thing is very mysterious. However, the police have every hope of laying their hands on the two others very shortly."

"They're always optimistic, aren't they?" returned Hugh. "Pity no one saw these blighters running round and throwing bombs about the house."

"That is just the fortunate thing, Captain Drummond," said the other mildly. "Far be it from me to desire vengeance on any man, but in this case I feel it is deserved. The unfortunate clerk downstairs who was brutally assaulted by them has confided to his employer that he believes he knows who one of the other two was. A huge man, Captain Drummond, of enormous strength: a man—well, really, do you know?—a man I should imagine just like you, and a man, who, popular rumour has it, is the head of a mysterious body calling itself the Black Gang. So that should prove a valuable clue for the police when they hear of it."

Not by a flicker of an eyelid did Drummond's face change as he listened with polite attention to the clergyman's remarks. But now once again his brain was moving quickly as he took in this new development. One card, at any rate, was down on the table: his identity as leader of the Black Gang was known to Peterson. It was the girl who had found him out: that was obvious. The point was how did it affect matters.

"An elusive person, I believe," he remarked quietly. "We've heard quite a lot of him in the papers recently. In fact, I was actually in Sir Bryan Johnstone's office when a gentleman of the name of Charles Latter came and demanded protection from the Black Gang."

For a moment a gleam of amazement shone in the other's eye.

"You surprise me," he murmured. "I trust it was afforded him."

Hugh waved a vast hand.

"Do you doubt it, Mr. Longmoor? I personally accompanied him to a house-party to ensure his safety. But as I told old Tum-tum afterwards—that's Sir Bryan Johnstone, you know, a great pal of mine—nothing that I could do could avert the catastrophe. I prattled to him gently, but it was no good. He went mad, Mr. Longmoor—quite, quite mad. The boredom of that house-party unhinged his brain. Have another chop?"

"How very extraordinary!" remarked the clergyman. "And what did your friend—er—Tum-tum say when he heard of the results of your supervision?"

"Well, quite unofficially, Mr. Longmoor, I think he was rather pleased. Latter was an unpleasant man, engaged in unpleasant work, and he does less harm when insane. A merciful thing, wasn't it, that we found such a suitable gathering of guests at our disposal?"

"And yet," pursued the Reverend Theodosius, "it struck me from an English paper I happened to pick up in Paris a little while ago, that the leader of this obscure gang claimed in some way to be responsible for the condition of Mr. Latter. He issued a ridiculous sort of manifesto to the Press, didn't he?"

"I believe he did," answered Drummond, draining his glass. "An effusion which ended with a threat to the people at the back of men like Latter. As if it would have any effect! Scum like that, Mr. Longmoor, remain hidden. They blush unseen. I do wish you'd have another chop."

"Thank you—no." The Reverend Theodosius waved away the waiter and leaned back in his chair. "Doubtless you are right, Captain Drummond, in championing this person; but if what this wretched, ill-treated clerk says is correct, I am afraid I can look on him as nothing less than a common thief. Of course, he may have made a mistake, but he seems very positive that one of the miscreants last night was the leader of the Black Gang himself."

"I see," said Drummond, with the air of a man on whom a great truth had dawned. "That hundred thick 'uns still rankling in the grey matter what time the vestry collapses."

"Hardly that," returned the clergyman severely. "My friend, whose office was wrecked, was amongst other things a dealer in precious stones. Last night in his desk were six magnificent diamonds—entrusted to him for sale by a—well, I will be discreet—by a well-known Russian nobleman. This morning he finds them gone—vanished—his room wrecked. Why, my heart bleeds for him."

"I'll bet it does," answered Drummond sympathetically. "Darned careless, isn't it, the way some of these people drop bombs about the place? Still, if your pal circulates an exact description of the diamonds to the police, he'll probably get 'em back in time. I suppose," he added by way of an afterthought, "I suppose he can go to the police about it?"

"I don't quite understand you, Captain Drummond." The Reverend Theodosius stared at his host in surprise.

"One never knows, these days, does one?" said Hugh mildly. "Dreadful thing to get a nice little bunch of diamonds shot at one's head, and then find you've got stolen property. It puts the next fellow who pinches them rather on velvet. A cup of coffee, won't you?"

"Fortunately nothing of that sort exists in this case. Yes, thank you, I would like some coffee."

"Good," said Hugh, giving the order to the waiter. "So that all you've got to do—or rather your pal—is to tell the police that the office was blown up by the leader of the Black Gang, and that the diamonds were pinched by the leader of the Black Gang, and that you would like his head on a silver salver by Wednesday week. It seems too easy to me. Cigarette? Turkish this side—gaspers the other."

"Thank you." The Reverend Theodosius helped himself from the case Hugh was holding out. "It certainly does seem easy, the way you put it."

"The only small trifle which seems to jut out from an otherwise clear-cut horizon is too ridiculous to worry about."

"And that is?"

"Why—who is the leader of the Black Gang? It would be a dreadful affair if they brought the wrong bird's head on a charger. No diamonds; no Bradburys; no nothing."

"I don't anticipate that it should be hard to discover that, Captain Drummond," said the clergyman mildly. "Surely with your marvellous police system——"

"And yet, Mr. Longmoor," said Hugh gravely, "even though lately I have been reinforcing that system—literally helping them myself—they are still completely in the dark as to his identity."

"Incredible," cried the other. "Still we can only hope for the best. By the way, I'm afraid your wife has finally deserted you for lunch." He pushed back his chair. "I shall hope to have the pleasure of making her acquaintance some other day. And now if you will excuse me, I must run away. My correspondence at the moment with regard to the relief funds for destitute Austrians is very voluminous. A thousand thanks for a most enjoyable meal."

He bowed with a courteous smile, and threaded his way through the crowded restaurant towards the door. And it was not until he had finally disappeared from sight that Hugh turned to Peter Darrell with a thoughtful expression on his face.

"Deuced interesting position of affairs, Peter," he remarked, lighting another cigarette. "He knows I'm the leader of our bunch, and doesn't know I know it; I know he's Peterson, and he doesn't know I know it; I wonder how long it will be before the gloves come off."

"Supposing he keeps out of it himself, and gives you away to the police," said Peter. "It'll be rather awkward, old son."

"Supposing he does, it would be," grinned Hugh. "I'd love to see Tum-tum's face. But, my dear old Peter, hasn't your vast brain grasped the one essential fact, that that is precisely what he can't do until he's certain I haven't got the diamonds? Apart altogether from a variety of very awkward disclosures about Number 5, Green Street—he, or his hunchback friend, would have to explain how they gained possession in the first place of those stones. I made discreet inquiries this morning, Peter, and that rose-pink diamond was one of the Russian Crown jewels. Awkward—very."

He smiled and ordered two brandies.

"Very, very awkward, Peter—but with distinct elements of humour. And I'm inclined to think the time is approaching when the seconds get out of the ring."

12

In which Count Zadowa is introduced to "Alice in Wonderland"

A quarter of an hour later the two young men stepped into Piccadilly. Evidently Phyllis was not proposing to turn up, and nothing was to be gained by remaining. The next move lay with the other side, and until it was played it was merely a question of marking time. At the entrance to the Ritz they separated, Peter turning eastwards to keep some mysterious date with a female minor star of theatrical London, while Hugh strolled along Berkeley Street towards his house. At times a faint smile crossed his face at the thought of Peterson devoting his young brain to the matter of starving Austrians, but for the most part a portentous frown indicated thought. For the life of him he couldn't see what was going to happen next. It appeared to him that the air wanted clearing; that in military parlance the situation was involved. And it was just as he was standing in Berkeley Square waving his stick vaguely as a material aid to thought, that he felt a touch on his arm.

"Excuse me, sir," said a voice at his elbow, "but I would like a few words with you."

He looked down, and his eyes narrowed suddenly. Standing beside him was the hunchback, Mr. Atkinson, and for a moment Hugh regarded him in silence. Then, dismissing a strong inclination to throw this unexpected apparition under a passing furniture van, he raised his eyebrows slightly and removed his cigar from his mouth. Evidently the next move had begun, and he felt curious as to what form it would take.

"My powers as a conversationalist are well known," he remarked, "amongst a large and varied circle. I was not, however, aware that you belonged to it. In other words, sir, who the deuce are you and what the dickens do you want to talk to me about?"

"Something which concerns us both very intimately," returned the other. "And with regard to the first part of your question—do you think it necessary to keep up the pretence, especially as there are no witnesses present? I suggest, however, that as our conversation may be a trifle prolonged, and this spot is somewhat draughty, we should adjourn to your house; Brook Street, I believe, is where you live, Captain Drummond."

Hugh removed his cigar, and stared at the hunchback thoughtfully.

"I haven't the slightest wish to have a prolonged conversation with you in any place, draughty or otherwise," he remarked at length. "However, if you are prepared to run the risk of being slung out of the window if you bore me, I'll give you ten minutes."

He turned on his heel and strolled slowly on towards his house, while the hunchback, shooting venomous glances at him from time to time, walked by his side in silence. And it was not until some five minutes later when they were both in Drummond's study that any further remark was made.

It was Hugh who spoke, standing with his back to the fireplace, and looking down on the misshapen little man who sat in an arm-chair facing the light. An unpleasant customer, he reflected, now that he saw him close to for the first time: a dangerous, vindictive little devil—but able, distinctly able. Just such a type as Peterson would choose for a tool.

"What is it you wish to say to me?" he said curtly.

"A few things, Captain Drummond," returned the other, "that may help to clear the air. In the first place may I say how pleased I am to make your acquaintance in the flesh, so to speak? I have long wanted a little talk with the leader of the Black Gang."

"I trust," murmured Hugh solicitously, "that the sun hasn't proved too much for you."

"Shall we drop this beating about the bush?" snapped the other.

"I shall drop you down the stairs if you talk to me like that, you damned little microbe," said Hugh coldly, and the other got to his feet with a snarl. His eyes, glaring like those of an angry cat, were fixed on Drummond, who suddenly put out a vast hand to screen the lower part of the hunchback's face. With a cry of fear he recoiled, and Hugh smiled grimly. So it had been Mr. Atkinson himself who had flung the bomb the night before: the eyes that had glared at him through the crack in the door were unmistakably the same as those he had just looked into over his own hand. With the rest of the face blotted out to prevent distraction there could be no doubt about it, and he was still smiling grimly as he lowered his hand.

"So you think I'm the leader of the Black Gang, do you?" he remarked. "I don't know that I'm very interested in your thoughts."

"I don't think: I know," said the hunchback viciously. "I found it out to-day."

"Indeed," murmured Hugh politely. "Would it be indiscreet to ask how you found out this interesting fact?"

"Do you deny it?" demanded the other furiously.

"My dear little man," said Hugh, "if you said I was the Pope I wouldn't deny it. All I ask is that now you've afflicted me with your presence you should amuse me. What are your grounds for this somewhat startling statement?"

"My grounds are these," said the hunchback, recovering his self-control: "last night my office in Hoxton was wrecked by a bomb."

"Good Lord!" interrupted Hugh mildly, "it must be old Theodosius Longmoor and his hundred quid. I thought he looked at me suspiciously during lunch."

"It was wrecked by a bomb, Captain Drummond," continued the other, not heeding the interruption. "That bomb also killed a man."

"It did," agreed Hugh grimly.

"One of the three men who broke in. The other two escaped—how I don't know. But one of them was recognized by the clerk downstairs."

"I gathered that was the story," said Hugh.

"He was recognized as the leader of the Black Gang," continued the hunchback. "And that was all until to-day. Just the leader of the Black Gang—an unknown person. But to-day—at the Ritz, Captain Drummond—my clerk, who had brought me a message, recognized him again, without his disguise. No longer an unknown man, you understand—but you."

Drummond smiled, and selected a cigarette from his case.

"Very pretty," he answered, "but a trifle crude. As I understand you, I gather that your shrewd and intelligent clerk states that the leader of the Black Gang broke into your office last night in order to indulge in the doubtful pastime of throwing bombs about the premises. He further states that I am the humorist in question. Allowing for the moment that your clerk is sane, what do you propose to do about it?"

"In certain eventualities, Captain Drummond, I propose to send an anonymous letter to Scotland Yard. Surprised though they would be to get it, it might help them to clear up the mystery of Mr. Latter's insanity. It may prove rather unpleasant for you, of course, but that can't be helped."

"It's kind of you to give me a loophole of escape," said Drummond pleasantly. "What are the eventualities to which you allude?"

"The non-return to me of a little bag containing diamonds," remarked the hunchback quietly. "They were in the desk which was wrecked by the bomb."

"Dear, dear," said Hugh. "Am I supposed to have them in my possession?"

"I can only hope most sincerely for your sake that you have," returned the other. "Otherwise I'm afraid that letter will go to the police."

For a while Drummond smoked in silence: then, with a lazy smile on his face, he sat down in an armchair facing the hunchback.

"Most interesting," he drawled. "Most interesting and entertaining. I'm not very quick, Mr.——, I've forgotten under what name you inflict yourself on a long-suffering world, but I shall call you Snooks—I'm not, as I say, very quick, Snooks, but as far as my brain can grapple with the problem it stands thus. If I give you back a packet of diamonds which I may, or may not, possess, you will refrain from informing the police that I am the leader of the Black Gang. If, on the contrary, I do not give them back to you, you will send them that interesting piece of information by means of an anonymous letter." The smile grew even lazier. "Well, you damned little excrescence, I call your bluff. Get on with it."

With a snarl of rage the hunchback snatched up his hat and rose to his feet.

"You call it bluff, do you?"—and his voice was shaking with fury. "Very good, you fool—I accept. And you'll be sorry when you see my cards."

"Sit down, Snooks: I haven't finished with you yet." There was still the same maddening smile on Drummond's face, which disappeared suddenly as the hunchback moved towards the door. In two strides Hugh had him by the collar, and with a force that made his teeth rattle Mr. Atkinson found himself back in his chair.

"I said sit down, Snooks," said Drummond pleasantly. "Don't let me have to speak to you again, or I might hurt you. There are one or two things I have to say to you before depriving myself of the pleasure of your company. By the post following the one which carries your interesting disclosure will go another letter addressed to Sir Bryan Johnstone himself. I shall be in the office when he opens it—and we shall both be roaring with laughter over the extraordinary delusion that I—quite the biggest fool of his acquaintance—could possibly be the leader of the Black Gang. And, as if to prove the utter absurdity of the suggestion, this second letter will be from the leader of the Black Gang himself. In it he will state that he was present at 5, Green Street, Hoxton, last night, in an endeavour to obtain possession of the anarchist and Bolshevist literature stored there. That he took with him a professional burglar to assist him in opening the safe and other things which might be there, and that while engaged in this eminently virtuous proceeding he found that he was trapped in the room by some mechanical device. And then, Snooks, will come a very interesting disclosure. He will state how suddenly he saw through a crack in the door a pair of eyes looking at him. And their colour—see, what is the colour of your eyes, Snooks?—grey-blue, very noticeable. Much the same as old Longmoor's—though his are a little bluer. And then the owner of the eyes, Snooks, was so inconsiderate as to throw a bomb in the room; a bomb which killed one of the men, and wrecked the desk. So that the owner of the eyes, Snooks, grey-blue eyes just like yours, is a murderer—a common murderer. And we hang men in England for murder." He paused and stared at the hunchback. "This is a jolly game, isn't it?"

"And you really imagine," said the hunchback contemptuously, "that even your police would believe such a story that a man would wreck his own office, when on your own showing he had the men trapped inside it."

"Probably not," said Drummond affably. "Any more than that they would believe that I was the leader of the Black Gang. So since they're such a wretched crowd of unbelievers I don't think it's much good playing that game, Snooks. Waste of time, isn't it? So I vote we play another one, all on our own—a little game of make-believe——like we used to play in the nursery."

"I haven't an idea what you're talking about, Captain Drummond," said the hunchback, shifting uneasily in his chair. For all trace of affability had vanished from the face of the man opposite him, to be replaced by an expression which made Mr. Atkinson pass his tongue once or twice over lips that had suddenly gone dry.

"Haven't you, you rat?" said Drummond quietly. "Then I'll tell you. Just for the next five minutes we're going to pretend that these two astonishing statements which the police—stupid fellows—won't believe are true. We're going to pretend—only pretend, mind you, Snooks—that I am the leader of the Black Gang; and we're going to pretend that you are the man who flung the bomb last night. Just for five minutes only, then we go back to reality and unbelieving policemen."

And if during the following five minutes strange sounds were heard by Denny in the room below, he was far too accustomed to the sounds of breaking furniture to worry. It wasn't until the hunchback pulled a knife that Drummond warmed to his work, but from that moment he lost his temper. And because the hunchback was a hunchback—though endowed withal by Nature with singular strength—it jarred on Drummond to fight him as if he had been a normal man. So he flogged him with a rhinoceros-hide whip till his arm ached, and then he flung him into a chair, gasping, cursing, and scarcely human.

"You shouldn't be so realistic in your stories, Snooks," he remarked affably, though his eyes were still merciless as he looked at the writhing figure. "And I feel quite sure that that is what the leader of the Black Gang would have done if he had met the peculiar humorist who threw that bomb last night. Bad habit—throwing bombs."

With a final curse the hunchback staggered to his feet, and his face was diabolical in its fury.

"You shall pay for that, Captain Drummond, stroke by stroke, and lash by lash," he said in a shaking voice.

Drummond laughed shortly.

"All the same old patter," he remarked. "Tell old Longmoor with my love——" He paused and grinned. "No, on second thoughts I think I'll tell his reverence myself—at the appointed time."

"What will you tell him?" sneered the hunchback.

"Why, that his church isn't the only place where dry-rot has set in. It's prevalent amongst his pals as well. Must you go? Straight down the stairs, and the card tray in the hall is only electro-plate—so you might leave it."

With a great effort Mr. Atkinson pulled himself together. His shoulders were still aching abominably from the hiding Drummond had given him, but his loss of self-control had been due more to mental than to physical causes. Immensely powerful though Drummond was, his clothes had largely broken the force of the blows for the hunchback. And now as he stood by the door the uppermost thought in his mind was that he had failed utterly and completely in the main object of the interview. He had come, if possible, to get the diamonds, and failing that, to find out for certain whether Drummond had them in his possession or not. And the net result had been a flogging and nothing more. Too late he realized that in dealing with men of the type of Hugh Drummond anything in the nature of a threat is the surest guarantee of a thick ear obtainable: but then Mr. Atkinson was not used to dealing with men of that type. And the uppermost thought in his mind at the moment was not how he could best revenge himself on this vast brute who had flogged him, but what he was going to say to the Reverend Theodosius Longmoor when he got back to the Ritz. The question of revenge could wait till later.

"Can we come to an understanding, Captain Drummond?" he remarked quietly. "I can assure you, of course, that you have made a terrible mistake in thinking that it was I who threw that bomb at you last night."

"At me?" Drummond laughed shortly. "Who said you'd thrown it at me? That wasn't the game at all, Snooks. You threw it at the leader of the Black Gang."

"Can't we put our cards on the table?" returned the other with studied moderation. "I know that you are that leader, you know it—though it is possible that no one else would believe it. I was wrong to threaten you—I should have known better; I apologize. But if I may say so I have had my punishment. Now as man to man—can we come to terms?"

"I am waiting," said Hugh briefly. "Kindly be as concise as possible."

"Those diamonds, Captain Drummond. Rightly or wrongly I feel tolerably certain that you either have them in your possession, or that you know where they are. Now those diamonds were not mine—did you speak? No. Well—to resume. The diamonds were not mine; they had been deposited in the desk in my office unknown to me. Then this fool—whom you foolishly think was myself—threw the bomb into the office to kill you. I admit it; he told me all about it. He did not kill you, for which fact, if I may say so, I am very glad. You're a sportsman, and you've fought like a sportsman—but our fight, Captain Drummond, has been over other matters. The diamonds are a side-show and hardly concern you and me. I'll be frank with you; they are the sole wealth saved by a Russian nobleman from the Bolshevist outrages. He deposited them in my office during my absence, with the idea of my selling them for him—and now he and his family must starve. And so what I propose is———"

"I don't think I want to hear your proposal, Snooks," said Drummond kindly. "Doubtless I look a fool; doubtless I am a fool, but I like to think that I'm not a congenital idiot. I'm glad you have discovered that it's not much use threatening me; but to tell you the strict truth, I prefer threats to nauseating hypocrisy. So much so in fact that the thought of that starving nobleman impels me to take more exercise. Ever read *Alice in Wonderland*, Snooks? A charming book—a masterpiece of English literature. And there is one singularly touching, not to say fruity, bit which concerns Father William—and a genteel young man."

With a look of complete bewilderment on his face Mr. Atkinson felt himself propelled through the door, until he came to a halt at the top of the stairs.

"It's a little poem, Snooks, and some day I will recite it to you. Just now I can only remember the one beautiful line which has suggested my new form of exercise."

Mr. Atkinson became aware of a boot in the lower portion of his back, and then the stairs seemed to rise up and hit him. He finally came to rest in the hall against an old oak chest of the pointed-corner type, and for a moment or two he lay there dazed. Then he scrambled to his feet to find three young men, who had emerged from a lower room during his flight, gazing at him impassively: while standing at the top of the stairs down which he had just descended, and outlined against a window, was the huge, motionless figure of Drummond. Half cursing, half sobbing, he staggered to the front door and opened it. Once more he looked back—not one of the four men had moved. They were just staring at him in absolute silence, and, with a sudden feeling of pure terror, Count Zadowa, *alias* Mr. Atkinson, shut the door behind him and staggered into the sunlit street.

13

In which Hugh Drummond and

the Reverend Theodosius have a little chat

"Come up, boys," laughed Hugh. "The fog of war is lifting slowly."

He led the way back into the study, and the other three followed him.

"That object, Ted, you will be pleased to hear, is the humorist who threw the bomb at us last night."

"The devil it was," cried Jerningham. "I hope you gave him something for me. Incidentally, how did he run you to earth here?"

"Things have moved within the last two or three hours," answered Drummond slowly. "Who do you think is stopping at the Ritz at the present moment? Who do you think lunched with Peter and me to-day? Why—Peterson, my buckos—no more and no less."

"Rot!" said Toby Sinclair incredulously.

"No more and no less. Peterson himself—disguised as a clergyman called Longmoor. And with him is dear Irma encased in woollen garments. And it was Irma who spotted the whole thing. I never recognized her, and she was sitting next to Peter and me in the lounge when we were discussing things. Of course, they're mixed up with that swab I've just kicked down the stairs—in fact we've bolted the fox. The nuisance of it is that by putting two and two together they've spotted me as the leader of our bunch. How I don't quite know, but they indubitably have. They also think I've got those diamonds: hence the visit of the hunchback, who did not know they were in the desk when he bunged the bomb. In fact, things are becoming clearer all the way round."

"I'm glad you think so," remarked Algy. "I'm dashed if I see it."

Drummond thoughtfully filled himself a glass of beer from the cask in the corner.

"Clearer, Algy—though not yet fully luminous with the light of day. Between Peterson and those diamonds there is, or was, a close and tender connection. I'll eat my hat on that. Between Peterson and the hunchback there is also a close connection—though I have my doubts if it's tender. And then there's me tripping lightly like the good fairy.... Hullo! What's this?"

He had opened his desk as he spoke, and was now staring fixedly at the lock.

"It's been forced," he said grimly. "Forced since this morning. They've been over this desk while I've been out. Push the bell, Ted."

They waited in silence till Denny appeared in answer to the ring.

"Someone has been in this room, Denny," said Drummond. "Someone has forced this desk since half-past eleven this morning."

"There's been no one in the house, sir," answered Denny, "except the man who came about the electric light."

"Electric grandmother," snapped his master. "You paralytic idiot, why did you leave him alone?"

"Well, sir, Mrs. Drummond was in the house at the time—and the servants were all round the place." Denny looked and felt aggrieved, and after a while Drummond smiled.

"What sort of man was it, you old fathead?"

"A very respectable sort of man," returned Denny with dignity. "I remarked to Mrs. Denny how respectable he was, sir. Why, he actually went some distance down the street to call a taxi for Mrs. Drummond to go to the Ritz...."

His words died away, as he stared in amazement at the expression on his master's face.

"What the devil is it, Hugh?" cried Ted Jerningham.

"He called a taxi, you say?" muttered Drummond. "The man who came here called a taxi?"

"Yes, sir," answered Denny. "He was leaving the house at the same time, and as there was none in sight he said he'd send one along at once."

"And Mrs. Drummond went in the taxi he sent?"

"Certainly, sir," said Denny in surprise. "To the Ritz, to join you. I gave the order myself to the driver."

The veins were standing out on Drummond's forehead, and for a moment it seemed as if he was going to hit his servant. Then with an effort he controlled himself, and sank back in his chair with a groan.

"It's all right, Denny," he said hoarsely. "It's not your fault: you couldn't have known. But—what a fool I've been! All this time wasted, when I might have been doing something."

"But what on earth's happened?" cried Algy.

"She never turned up at the Ritz, Algy: Phyllis never turned up for lunch. At first I thought she was late, and we waited. Then I thought she'd run into some pal and had gone to feed somewhere else. And then, what with talking to Peterson, and later that hunchback, I forget all about her."

"But, good heavens, Hugh, what do you mean?" said Ted. "You don't think that———"

"Of course I think it. I know it. They've got her: they've kidnapped her. Right under my nose." He rose and began to pace up and down the room with long, uneven strides, while the others watched him anxiously.

"That dammed girl heard me say that she was coming to lunch, and just after that she went upstairs. And Peterson, being Peterson, took a chance—and he's pulled it off."

"Ring up Scotland Yard, man," cried Toby Sinclair.

"What the devil am I to tell them? They'd think I was off my head. And I've got no proof that Peterson is at the bottom of it. I haven't even got any proof that would convince them that Longmoor is Peterson."

Algy Longworth stood up, serious for once in a way.

"There's no time now to beat about the bush, Hugh. If they've got Phyllis there's only one possible thing that you can do. Go straight to Bryan Johnstone and put all your cards on the table. Tell him the whole thing from A to Z—conceal nothing. And then leave the matter in his hands. He won't let you down."

For a moment or two Hugh faced them undecided. The sudden danger to Phyllis seemed to have robbed him temporarily of his power of initiative; for the time he had ceased to be the leader.

"Algy's right," said Jerningham quietly. "It doesn't matter a damn what happens to us, you've got to think about Phyllis. We'll get it in the neck—but there was always that risk."

"I believe you're right," muttered Hugh, looking round for his hat. "My brain's all buzzing, I can't think——"

And at that moment the telephone bell rang on his desk.

"Answer it, Ted," said Hugh.

Jerningham picked up the receiver.

"Yes—this is Captain Drummond's house. No—it's not him speaking. Yes—I'll give him any message you like. Who are you? Who? Mr. Longmoor at the Ritz. I see. Yes—he told me you had lunched with him to-day. Oh! yes, certainly."

For a while Ted Jerningham stood holding the receiver to his ear, and only the thin, metallic voice of the speaker at the other end broke the silence of the room. It went on, maddeningly indistinct to the three men crowding round the instrument, broken only by an occasional monosyllable from Jerningham. Then with a final—"I will certainly tell him," Ted laid down the instrument.

"What did he say, Ted?" demanded Hugh agitatedly.

"He sent a message to you, old man. It was approximately to this effect—that he was feeling very uneasy because your wife had not turned up at lunch, and that he hoped there had been no accident. He further went on to say that since he had parted from you a most peculiar piece of information had come to his knowledge, which, incredible though it might appear seemed to bear on her failure to turn up at the Ritz. He most earnestly begged that you should go round and see him at once—because if his information was correct any delay might prove most dangerous for her. And lastly, on no account were you to go to the police until you had seen him."

For a while there was silence in the room. Drummond, frowning heavily, was staring out of the window; the others, not knowing what to say, were waiting for him to speak. And after a while he swung round, and they saw that the air of indecision had gone.

"That simplifies matters considerably," he said quietly. "It reduces it to the old odds of Peterson and me."

"But you'll go to the police, old man," cried Algy. "You won't pay any attention to that message. He'll never know that you haven't come straight to him."

Drummond laughed shortly.

"Have you forgotten the rules so much, Algy, that you think that? Look out of the window, man, only don't be seen. There's a fellow watching the house now—I couldn't go a yard without Peterson knowing. Moreover I'm open to a small bet that he knew I was in the house when he was talking to Ted. Good heavens! No. Peterson is not the sort of man to play those monkey-tricks with. He's got Phyllis, the whole thing is his show. And if I went to the police, long before they could bring it home to him, or get her back—she'd be—why"—and once again the veins stood out on his forehead—"Lord knows what the swine wouldn't have done to her. It's just a barter at the present moment—the diamonds against her. And there's to be no haggling. They win the first round—but there are a few more on the horizon."

"What are you going to do?" said Ted.

"Exactly what he suggests," answered Hugh. "Go round and see him at the Ritz—now, at once. I shan't take the diamonds with me, but there will be no worry over the exchange as far as I'm concerned. It's just like his dirty method of fighting to go for a girl," he finished savagely.

"You don't think they've hurt Mrs. Drummond, sir," said Denny anxiously.

"If they have, they'll find the remains of an elderly parson in Piccadilly," returned Hugh, as he slipped a small revolver into his pocket. "But I don't think so. Carl is far too wise to do anything so stupid as that. He's tried with the hunchback and failed, now he's trying this. And he wins."

He crossed to the door and opened it.

"In case I don't come back by six, the diamonds are in my sponge bag in the bathroom—and go straight to Scotland Yard. Tell Tum-tum the whole yarn."

With a brief nod he was gone, and a moment later he was in the street. It was almost deserted, and he waited on the pavement for the loitering gentleman who came obsequiously forward.

"Taxi, sir?"

A convenient one—an almost too convenient one—came to a standstill beside them, and Hugh noticed a quick look flash between the driver and the other man. Then he took stock of the taxi, and behold it was not quite as other taxis. And in his mind arose an unholy desire. As has been said, the street was nearly deserted, and it was destined to become even more deserted. There was a crash of breaking glass and the loiterer disappeared through one window of the machine.

Hugh stared at the astounded driver.

"If you say one word, you appalling warthog," he remarked gently, "I'll throw you through the other."

It was a happy omen, and he felt better as he walked towards the Ritz. Simple and direct—that was the game. No more tortuous intrigues for him; hit first and apologize afterwards. And he was still in the same mood when he was shown into the sitting-room where the Reverend Theodosius Longmoor was busily working on Austrian famine accounts. He rose as Hugh entered, and his daughter, still knitting busily, gave him a charming girlish smile.

"Ah! my dear young friend," began Mr. Longmoor, "I see you've had my message."

"Yes," answered Hugh affably, "I was standing next door to the fellow you were talking to. But before we come to business, so to speak—I must really ask you not to send Snooks round again. I don't like him. Why, my dear Carl, I preferred our late lamented Henry Lakington."

There was a moment of dead silence, during which the Reverend Theodosius stared at him speechlessly and the busy knitter ceased to knit. The shock was so complete and sudden that even Carl Peterson seemed at a loss, and Drummond laughed gently as he took a chair.

"I'm tired of this dressing-up business, Carl," he remarked in the same affable voice. "And it's so stupid to go on pretending when everybody knows. So I thought we might as well have all the cards on the table. Makes the game much easier."

He selected a cigarette with care, and offered his case to the girl.

"My most hearty congratulations, mademoiselle," he continued. "I may say that it was not you I recognized, but your dear—it is father still, isn't it? And now that we've all met again you must tell me some time how you got away last year."

But by this time the clergyman had found his voice.

"Are you mad, sir?" he spluttered. "Are you insane? How dare you come into this room and insult my daughter and myself? I shall ring the bell, sir, and have you removed."

He strode across the room, and Drummond watched him calmly.

"I've just called one bluff this afternoon, Carl," he said lazily. "Now I'll call another. Go on, push the bell. Send for the police and say I've insulted you. Go and see dear old Tum-tum yourself: he'll be most awfully braced at meeting you."

The other's hand fell slowly to his side, and he looked at his daughter with a resigned expression in his face.

"Really, my dear, I think that the heat—or perhaps——" He paused expressively, and Drummond laughed.

"You were always a good actor, Carl, but is it worth while? There are no witnesses here, and I'm rather pressed for time. There's no good pretending that it's the heat or that I'm tight, because I'm the only member of the audience, and you can't deceive me, you really can't. Through a series of accidents you have become aware of the fact that I am the leader of the Black Gang. You can go and tell the police if you like—in fact, that horrible little man who came round to see me threatened to do so. But if you do, I shall tell them who you are, and I shall also inform them of the secret history of the bomb. So that, though it will be awkward for me, Carl, it will be far more awkward for you and Mademoiselle Irma; and it will be positively unhealthy for Snooks. You take me so far, don't you? Up to date I have been dealing in certainties; now we come to contingencies. It strikes me that there are two doubtful points, old friend of my youth—just two. And those two points are the whereabouts respectively of my wife and your diamonds. Now, Carl, do we talk business or not?"

"My dear young man," said the other resignedly, "I intended to talk business with you when you arrived if you had given me a chance. But as you've done nothing but talk the most unmitigated drivel since you've come into the room I haven't had a chance. You appear obsessed with the absurd delusion that I am some person called Carl, and—— But where are you going?"

Drummond paused at the door.

"I am going straight to Scotland Yard. I shall there tell Sir Bryan Johnstone the whole story from A to Z, at the same time handing him a little bag containing diamonds which has recently come into my possession."

"You admit you've got them," snapped the other, letting the mask drop for a moment.

"That's better, Carl—much better." Drummond came back into the room. "I admit I've got them—but they're in a place where you can never find them, and they will remain there until six o'clock to-night, when they go straight to Scotland Yard—unless, Carl—unless my wife is returned to me absolutely unscathed and unhurt before that hour. It is five o'clock now."

"And if she is returned—what then?"

"You shall have the diamonds."

For a space the two men stared at one another in silence, and it was the girl who finally spoke.

"What proof have we that you'll keep your word?"

"Common sense," said Hugh quietly. "My wife is somewhat more valuable to me than a bagful of diamonds. In addition, you know me well enough to know that I do not break my word. Anyway, those are my terms—take them or leave them. But I warn you that should anything happen to her—nothing will prevent me going straight to the police. No consideration of unpleasant results for me will count even for half a second. Well, do you accept?"

"There is just one point, Captain Drummond," remarked the clergyman mildly. "Supposing that I am able to persuade certain people to—er—expedite the return of Mrs. Drummond in exchange for that little bag, where do you and I stand after the bargain is transacted. Do you still intend to tell the police of your extraordinary delusions with regard to me?"

"Not unless they should happen to become acquainted with the ridiculous hallucination that I am the leader of the Black Gang," answered Drummond. "That was for your ears alone, my little one, and as you knew it already you won't get fat on it, will you? No, my intentions—since we are having a heart-to-heart talk—are as follows. Once the exchange is effected we will start quite fair and square—just like last time, Carl. It doesn't pay you to go to the police: it doesn't pay me, so we'll have a single on our own. I am frightfully anxious to add you to my collection of specimens, and I can't believe you are burning with zeal to go. But we'll see, Carl, we'll see. Only—no more monkey-tricks with my wife. Don't let there be any misunderstanding on that point."

The clergyman smiled benevolently.

"How aptly you put things!" he murmured. "I accept your terms, and I shall look forward afterwards to the single on our own that you speak about. And now—as to details. You must bear in mind that just as Mrs. Drummond is more valuable to you than diamonds, she is also somewhat larger. In other words, it will be obvious at once whether those whom I represent have kept their side of the bargain by producing your wife. It will not be obvious whether you have kept yours. The diamonds may or may not be in your pocket, and once you have your wife in your arms again the incentive to return the diamonds would be diminished. So I suggest, Captain Drummond, that you should bring the diamonds to me—here in this room, before six o'clock as a proof of good faith. You may keep them in your possession; all that I require is to see them. I will then engage on my side to produce Mrs. Drummond within a quarter of an hour."

For a moment Drummond hesitated, fearing a trick. And yet it was a perfectly reasonable request, as he admitted to himself. From their point of view it was quite true that they could have no proof that he would keep his word, and once Phyllis was in the room there would be nothing to prevent the two of them quietly walking out through the door and telling the Reverend Theodosius to go to hell.

"Nothing can very well happen at the Ritz, can it?" continued the clergyman suavely. "And you see I am even trusting you to the extent that I do not actually ask you to hand over the diamonds until your wife comes. I have no guarantee that even then you will not get up and leave the room with them still in your possession. You are too big and strong a man, Captain Drummond, to allow of any horseplay—especially—er—in a clergyman's suite of rooms."

Drummond laughed. "Cut it out, Carl!" he exclaimed. "Cut it out, for heaven's sake! All right. I agree. I'll go round and get the stones now."

He rose and went to the door.

"But don't forget, Carl—if there are any monkey-tricks, heaven help you."

The door closed behind him, and with a snarl the clergyman spun round on the girl.

"How the devil has he spotted us?" His face was convulsed with rage. "He's the biggest fool in the world, and yet he spots me every time. However, there's no time to worry about that now; we must think."

He took one turn up and down the room, then he nodded his head as if he had come to a satisfactory decision. And when he spoke to the girl, who sat waiting expectantly on the sofa, he might have been the head of a big business firm giving orders to his managers for the day.

"Ring up headquarters of A branch," he said quietly. "Tell them to send round Number 13 to this room at once. He must be here within a quarter of an hour."

"Number 13," repeated the girl, making a note. "That's the man who is such a wonderful mimic, isn't it? Well?"

"Number 10 and the Italian are to come with him, and they are to wait below for further orders."

"That all?" She rose to her feet as the Reverend Theodosius crossed rapidly to the door which led to the bathroom. "What about that silly little fool—his wife?"

For a moment the man paused, genuine amazement on his face.

"My dear girl, you don't really imagine I ever intended to produce her, do you? And any lingering doubt I might have had on the matter disappeared the moment I found Drummond knew us. There's going to be no mistake this time over that young gentleman, believe me."

With a slight laugh he disappeared into the bathroom, and as little Janet put through her call a tinkling of bottles seemed to show that the Reverend Theodosius was not wasting time.

14

In which a Rolls-Royce runs amok

Some ten minutes later he emerged from the bathroom carefully carrying a saucer in his hand. The girl's announcement that Number 13 had started at once had been received with a satisfied grunt, but he had spoken no word. And the girl, glancing through the door, saw him with his shirt sleeves rolled up above his elbows, carefully mixing two liquids together and stirring the result gently with a glass rod. He was completely absorbed in his task, and with a faint smile on her face she went back to the sofa and waited. She knew too well the futility of speaking to him on such occasions. Even when he came in, carrying the result of his labours with a pair of india-rubber gloves on his hands, she made no remark, but waited for him to relieve her curiosity.

He placed the mixture on the table and glanced round the room. Then he pulled up one of the ordinary stuff arm-chairs to the table and removed the linen head-rest, which he carefully soaked with the contents of the saucer, dabbing the liquid on with a sponge, so as not to crumple the linen in any way. He used up all the liquid, and then, still with the same meticulous care, he replaced the head-rest on the chair, and stood back and surveyed his handiwork.

"Look all right?" he asked briefly.

"Quite," answered the girl. "What's the game?"

"Drummond has got to sit in that chair," he returned, removing the saucer and the sponge to the bathroom, and carefully peeling off his gloves. "He's got to sit in that chair, my dear, and afterwards that linen affair has got to be burnt. And whatever happens"—he paused for a moment in front of her—"don't you touch it."

Quietly and methodically, he continued his preparations, as if the most usual occurrence in the world was in progress. He picked up two other chairs, and carried them through into the bedroom; then he returned and placed an open dispatch-case with a sheaf of loose papers on another one.

"That more or less limits the seating accommodation," he remarked, glancing round the room. "Now if you, *cara mia*, will spread some of your atrocious woollen garments on the sofa beside you, I think we can guarantee the desired result."

But apparently his preparations were not over yet. He crossed to the sideboard and extracted a new and undecanted bottle of whisky. From this he withdrew about a dessertspoonful of the spirit, and replaced it with the contents of a small phial which he took out of his waistcoat pocket. Then he forced back the cork until it was right home, and with the greatest care replaced the cap of tinfoil round the top of the bottle. And the girl, coming over to where he was working, saw that the bottle was again as new.

"What a consummate artist you are, *chéri*!" she said, laying a hand on his shoulder.

The Reverend Theodosius smiled and passed his arm round her waist.

"One of the earliest essentials of our—er—occupation, my little one, is to learn how to insert dope into an apparently untouched bottle."

"But do you think you will get him to drink even out of a new bottle?"

"I hope so. I shall drink myself. But even if he doesn't, the preparation on the chair is the essential thing. Once his neck touches that——"

With an expressive wave of his hand he vanished once more into the bathroom, returning with his coat.

"Don't you remember that Italian toxicologist—Fransioli?" he remarked. "We met him in Naples three years ago, and he obligingly told me that he had in his possession the secret of one of the real Borgia poisons. I remember I had a most interesting discussion with him on the subject. The internal application is harmless; the external application is what matters. That acts alone, but if the victim can be induced to take it internally as well it acts very much better."

"Fransioli?" She frowned thoughtfully. "Wasn't that the name of the man who had the fatal accident on Vesuvius?"

"That's the fellow," answered the Reverend Theodosius, arranging a siphon and some glasses on a tray. "He persuaded me to ascend it with him, and on the way up he was foolish enough to tell me that the bottles containing this poison had been stolen from his laboratory. I don't know whether he suspected me or not—I was an Austrian Baron at the time, if I remember aright—but when he proceeded to peer over the edge of the crater at a most dangerous point I thought it better to take no risks. So—er—the accident occurred. And I gathered he was really a great loss to science."

He glanced at his watch, and the girl laughed delightedly.

"It will be interesting to see if his claims for it are true," he continued thoughtfully. "I have only used it once, but on that occasion I inadvertently put too much into the wine, and the patient died. But with the right quantities it produces—so he stated, and I saw him experiment on a dog—a type of partial paralysis, not only of the body, but of the mind. You can see, you can hear, but you can't speak and you can't move. What ultimately happens with a human being I don't know, but the dog recovered."

A quick double knock came at the door, and with one final glance round the room the Reverend Theodosius crossed to his desk and sat down.

"Come in," he called, and a small dapper-looking man entered.

"Number 13, sir," said the new-comer briefly, and the other nodded.

"I am expecting a man here shortly, 13," remarked the clergyman, "whose voice I shall want you to imitate over the telephone."

"Only over the telephone, sir?"

"Only over the telephone. You will not be able to be in this room, but there is a bathroom adjoining in which you can hear every word that is spoken." The other nodded as if satisfied. "For how long will you require to hear him talk?"

"Five or ten minutes, sir, will be ample."

"Good. You shall have that. There's the bathroom. Go in, and don't make a sound."

"Very good, sir."

"And wait. Have Giuseppi and Number 10 come yet?"

"They left headquarters, sir, just after I did. They should be here by now."

The man disappeared into the bathroom, closing the door behind him, and once again the Reverend Theodosius glanced at his watch.

"Our young friend should be here shortly," he murmured. "And then the single which he seems so anxious to play can begin in earnest."

The benign expression which he had adopted as part of his role disappeared for an instant to be replaced by a look of cold fury.

"The single will begin in earnest," he repeated softly, "and it's the last one he will ever play."

The girl shrugged her shoulders.

"He has certainly asked for it," she remarked, "but it strikes me that you had better be careful. You may bet on one thing—that he hasn't kept his knowledge about you and me to himself. Half those young idiots that run about behind him know everything by this time, and if they go to Scotland Yard it will be very unpleasant for us, *mon chéri*. And that they certainly will do if anything should happen to dear Hugh."

The clergyman smiled resignedly.

"After all these years, you think it necessary to say that to me! My dear, you pain me—you positively wound me to the quick. I will guarantee that all Drummond's friends sleep soundly in their beds to-night, harbouring none but the sweetest thoughts of the kindly and much-maligned old clergyman at the Ritz."

"And what of Drummond himself?" continued the girl.

"It may be to-night, or it may be to-morrow. But accidents happen at all times—and one is going to happen to him." He smiled sweetly, and lit a cigar. "A nasty, sticky accident which will deprive us of his presence. I haven't worried over the details yet—but doubtless the inspiration will come. And here, if I mistake not, is our hero himself."

The door swung open and Drummond entered.

"Well, Carl, old lad," he remarked breezily, "here I am on the stroke of time with the bag of nuts all complete."

"Excellent," murmured the clergyman waving a benevolent hand towards the only free chair. "But if you must call me by my Christian name, why not make it Theo?"

Drummond grinned delightedly.

"As you wish, my little one. Theo it shall be in future, and Janet." He bowed to the girl as he sat down. "There's just one little point I want to mention, Theo, before we come to the laughter and games. Peter Darrell, whom you may remember of old, and who lunched with us to-day, is sitting on the telephone in my house. And eight o'clock is the time limit. Should his childish fears for my safety and my wife's not be assuaged by that hour, he will feel compelled to interrupt Tum-tum at his dinner. I trust I make myself perfectly clear."

"You are the soul of lucidity," beamed the clergyman.

"Good! Then first of all, there are the diamonds. No, don't come too near, please; you can count them quite easily from where you are." He tumbled them out of the bag, and they lay on the table like great pools of liquid light. The girl's breath came quickly as she saw them, and Drummond turned on her with a smile.

"To one given up to good works and knitting, Janet, doubtless, such things do not appeal. Tell me, Theo," he remarked as he swept them back into the bag—"who was the idiot who put them in Snooks' desk? Don't answer if you'd rather not give away your maidenly secrets; but it was a pretty full-sized bloomer on his part, wasn't it—pooping off the old bomb?"

He leaned back in his chair, and for a moment a gleam shone in the other's eyes, for the nape of Drummond's neck came exactly against the centre of the impregnated linen cover.

"Doubtless, Captain Drummond, doubtless," he murmured politely. "But if you will persist in talking in riddles, don't you think we might choose a different subject until Mrs. Drummond arrives."

"Anything you like, Theo," said Drummond. "I'm perfectly happy talking about you. How the devil do you do it?" He sat up and stared at the other man with genuine wonder on his face. "Eyes different—nose—voice—figure—everything different. You're a marvel—but for that one small failing of yours."

"You interest me profoundly," said the clergyman. "What is this one small failing that makes you think I am other than what I profess to be?"

Drummond laughed genially.

"Good heavens, don't you know what it is? Hasn't Janet told you? It's that dainty little trick of yours of tickling the left ear with the right big toe that marks you every time. No man can do that, Theo, and blush unseen."

He leaned back again in his chair, and passed his hand over his forehead.

"By Jove, it's pretty hot in here, isn't it?"

"It is close everywhere to-day," answered the other easily, though his eyes behind the spectacles were fixed intently on Drummond. "Would you care for a drink?"

Drummond smiled; the sudden fit of muzziness seemed to have passed as quickly as it had come.

"Thank you—no," he answered politely. "In your last incarnation, Theo, you may remember that I did not drink with you. There is an element of doubt about your liquor which renders it a dangerous proceeding."

"As you will," said the clergyman indifferently, at the same time placing the bottle of whisky and the glasses on the table. "If you imagine that I am capable of interfering with an unopened bottle of Johnny Walker, obtained from the cellars of the Ritz, it would be well not to join me." He was carefully removing the tin foil as he spoke, and once again the strange muzzy feeling crept over Drummond. He felt as if things had suddenly become unreal—as if he was dreaming. His vision seemed blurred, and then for a second time it passed away, leaving only a strange mental confusion. What was he doing in this room? Who was this benevolent old clergyman drawing the cork out of a bottle of whisky?

With an effort he pulled himself together. It must be the heat or something, he reflected, and he must keep his brain clear. Perhaps a whisky-and-soda would help. After all, there could be no danger in drinking from a bottle which he had seen opened under his very eyes.

"Do you know, Theo," he remarked, "I think I will change my mind and have a whisky-and-soda."

His voice sounded strange to his ears; and he wondered if the others noticed anything. But apparently not; the clergyman merely nodded briefly, and remarked, "say when."

"When," said Drummond, with a foolish sort of laugh. It was a most extraordinary thing, but he couldn't focus his eyes; there were two glasses on the table and two clergymen splashing in soda from two siphons. Surely he wasn't going to faint; bad thing to faint when he was alone with Peterson.

He took a gulp at his drink and suddenly began to talk—foolishly and idiotically.

"Nice room, Carl, old lad.... Never expected meet you again: certainly not in nice room.... Wrote letter paper after poor old Latter went mad. Drew you—drew badger. Send badger mad too."

His voice trailed away, and he sat there blinking stupidly. Everything was confused, and his tongue seemed weighted with lead. He reached out again for his glass—or tried to—and his arm refused to move. And suddenly out of the jumble of thoughts in his brain there emerged the one damning certainty that somehow or other he had been trapped and drugged. He gave a hoarse, inarticulate cry, and struggled to rise to his feet, but it was useless; his legs and arms felt as if they were bound to the chair by iron bands. And in the mist that swam before his eyes he saw the mocking faces of the clergyman and his daughter.

"It seems to have acted most excellently," remarked the Reverend Theodosius, and Drummond found he could hear quite normally; also his sight was improving; things in the room seemed steadier. And his mind was becoming less confused—he could think again. But to move or to speak was utterly impossible; all he could do was to sit and watch and rage inwardly at having been such a fool as to trust Peterson.

But that gentleman appeared in no hurry. He was writing with a gold pencil on a letter pad, and every now and then he paused and smiled thoughtfully. At length he seemed satisfied, and crossed to the bathroom door.

"We are ready now," Drummond heard him say, and he wondered what was going to happen next. To turn his head was impossible; his range of vision was limited by the amount he could turn his eyes. And then, to his amazement, he heard his own voice speaking from somewhere behind him—not, perhaps, quite so deep, but an extraordinarily good imitation which would have deceived nine people out of ten when they could not see the speaker. And then he heard Peterson's voice again mentioning the telephone, and he realized what they were going to do.

"I want you," Peterson was saying, "to send this message that I have written down to that number—using this gentleman's voice."

They came into his line of vision, and the new arrival stared at him curiously. But he asked no questions—merely took the paper and read it through carefully. Then he stepped over to the telephone, and took off the receiver. And, helplessly impotent, Drummond sat in his chair and heard the following message spoken in his own voice:

"Is that you, Peter, old bird? I've made the most unholy bloomer. This old bloke Theodosius isn't Carl at all. He's a perfectly respectable pillar of the Church."

And then apparently Darrell said something, and Peterson, who was listening through the second ear-piece, whispered urgently to the man.

"Phyllis," he went on—"she's as right as rain! The whole thing is a boss shot of the first order...."

Drummond made another stupendous effort to rise, and for a moment everything went blank. Dimly he heard his own voice still talking into the instrument but he only caught a word here and there, and then it ceased, and he realized that the man had left the room. It was Peterson's voice close by him that cleared his brain again.

"I trust you approve of the way our single has started, Captain Drummond," he remarked pleasantly. "Your friend Peter, I am glad to say, is more than satisfied, and has announced his intention of dining with some female charmer. Also he quite understands why your wife has gone into the country—you heard that bit I hope, about her sick cousin?—and he realizes that you are joining her."

And suddenly the pleasant voice ceased, and the clergyman continued in a tone of cold, malignant fury.

"You rat! You damned interfering young swine! Now that you're helpless I don't mind admitting that I am the man you knew as Carl Peterson, but I'm not going to make the mistake he made a second time. I under-estimated you, Captain Drummond. I left things to that fool Lakington. I treated you as a blundering young ass, and I realized too late that you weren't such a fool as you looked. This time I am paying you the compliment of treating you as a dangerous enemy, and a clever man. I trust you are flattered."

He turned as the door opened, and the man who had telephoned came in with two others. One was a great, powerful-looking man who might have been a prize-fighter; the other was a lean, swarthy-skinned foreigner, and both of them looked unpleasant customers. And Hugh wondered what was going to happen next, while his eyes rolled wildly from side to side as if in search of some way of escape. It was like some ghastly nightmare when one is powerless to move before some dreadful figment of the brain, only to be saved at the last moment by waking up. Only in Hugh's case he was awake already, and the dream was reality.

He saw the men leave the room, and then Peterson came over to him again. First he took the little bag of diamonds out of his pocket, and it struck Hugh that though he had seen the other's hand go into his pocket, he had felt nothing. He watched Peterson and the girl as they examined the stones; he watched Peterson as he locked them up in a steel despatch-case. And then Peterson disappeared out of his range of vision. He was conscious that he was near him—just behind him—and the horror of the nightmare increased. It had been better when they were talking; at least then he could see them. But now, with both of them out of sight—hovering round the back of his chair, perhaps—and without a sound in the room save the faint hum of the traffic outside, the strain was getting unbearable.

And then another thought came to add to his misery. If they killed him—and they intended to, he was certain—what would happen to Phyllis?

They'd got her too, somewhere; what were they going to do to her? Again he made a superhuman effort to rise; again he failed so much as to move his finger. And for a while he raved and blasphemed mentally.

It was hopeless, utterly hopeless; he was caught like a rat in a trap.

And then he began to think coherently again. After all, they couldn't kill him here in the Ritz. You can't have dead men lying about in your room in an hotel. And they would have to move him some time; they couldn't leave him sitting there. How were they going to get him out? He couldn't walk, and to carry him out as he was would be impossible. Too many of the staff below knew him by sight.

Suddenly Peterson came into view again. He was in his shirt sleeves and was smoking a cigar, and Hugh watched him sorting out papers. He seemed engrossed in the matter, and paid no more attention to the hapless figure at the table than he did to the fly on the window. At length he completed his task, and having closed the dispatch-case with a snap, he rose and stood facing Hugh.

"Enjoying yourself?" he remarked. "Wondering what is going to happen? Wondering where dear Phyllis is?"

He gave a short laugh.

"Excellent drug that, isn't it? The first man I tried it on died—so you're lucky. You never felt me put a pin in the back of your arm, did you?"

He laughed again; in fact, the Reverend Theodosius seemed in an excellent temper.

"Well, my friend, you really asked for it this time, and I'm afraid you're going to get it. I cannot have someone continually worrying me like this, so I'm going to kill you, as I always intended to some day. It's a pity, and in many ways I regret it, but you must admit yourself that you really leave me no alternative. It will appear to be accidental, so you need entertain no bitter sorrow that I shall suffer in any way. And it will take place very soon—so soon, in fact, that I doubt if you will recover from the effects of the drug. I wouldn't guarantee it: you might. As I say, you are only the second person on whom I have tried it. And with regard to your wife—our little Phyllis—it may interest you to know that I have not yet made up my mind. I may find it necessary for her to share in your accident—or even to have one all on her own: I may not."

The raving fury in Drummond's mind as his tormentor talked on showed clearly in his eyes, and Peterson laughed.

"Our friend is getting quite agitated, my dear," he remarked, and the girl came into sight. She was smoking a cigarette, and for a while they stared at their helpless victim much as if he was a specimen in a museum.

"You're an awful idiot, my Hugh, aren't you?" she said at length. "And you have given us such a lot of trouble. But I shall quite miss you, and all our happy little times together."

She laughed gently, and glanced at the clock.

"They ought to be here fairly soon," she remarked. "Hadn't we better get him out of sight?"

Peterson nodded, and between them they pushed Drummond into the bathroom.

"You see, my friend," remarked Peterson affably, "it is necessary to get you out of the hotel without arousing suspicion. A simple little matter, but it is often the case that one trips up more over simple matters than over complicated ones."

He was carefully inserting a pin into his victim's leg as he spoke, and watching intently for any sign of feeling.

"Why, I remember once," he continued conversationally, "that I was so incredibly foolish as to replace the cork in a bottle of prussic acid after I had—er—compelled a gentleman to drink the contents. He was in bed at the time, and everything pointed to suicide, except that confounded cork. I mean, would any man, after he's drunk sufficient prussic acid to poison a regiment, go and cork up the empty bottle? It only shows how careful one must be over these little matters."

The girl put her head round the door.

"They're here," she remarked abruptly, and Peterson went into the other room, half closing the door. And Drummond, writhing impotently, heard the well-modulated voice of the Reverend Theodosius.

"Ah, my dear friend, my very dear old friend! What joy it is to see you again. I am greatly obliged to you for escorting this gentleman up personally."

"Not at all, sir, not at all! Would you care for dinner to be served up here?"

Someone to do with the hotel, thought Drummond, and he made one final despairing effort to move. He felt it was his last chance, and it failed—as the others had done before. And it seemed to him that the mental groan he gave must have been audible, so utterly beyond hope did he feel. But it wasn't; no sound came from the bathroom to the ears of the courteous sub-manager.

"I will ring later if I require it," Peterson was saying in his gentle, kindly voice. "My friend, you understand, is still on a very strict diet, and he comes to me more for spiritual comfort than for bodily. But I will ring should I find he would like to stay."

"Very good, sir."

And Drummond heard the door close, and knew that his last hope had gone.

Then he heard Peterson's voice again, sharp and incisive.

"Lock the door. You two—get Drummond. He's in the bathroom."

The two men he had previously seen entered, and carried him back into the sitting-room, where the whole scheme was obvious at a glance. Just getting out of an ordinary invalid's chair was a big man of more or less the same build as himself. A thick silk muffler partially disguised his face; a soft hat was pulled well down over his eyes, and Drummond realized that the gentleman who had been wheeled in for spiritual comfort would not be wheeled out.

The two men pulled him out of his chair, and then, forgetting his condition, they let him go, and he collapsed like a sack of potatoes on the floor, his legs and arms sprawling in grotesque attitudes.

They picked him up again, and not without difficulty they got him into the other man's overcoat; and finally they deposited him in the invalid's chair, and tucked him up with the rug.

"We will give it half an hour," remarked Peterson, who had been watching the operation. "By that time our friend will have had sufficient spiritual solace; and until then you two can wait outside. I will give you your full instructions later."

"Will you want me any more, sir?" The man whose place Drummond had taken was speaking.

"No," said Peterson curtly. "Get out as unostentatiously as you can. Go down by the stairs and not by the lift."

With a nod, he dismissed them all, and once again Drummond was alone with his two chief enemies.

"Simple, isn't it, my friend?" remarked Peterson. "An invalid arrives, and an invalid will shortly go. And once you've passed the hotel doors you will cease to be an invalid. You will become again that well-known young man about town—Captain Hugh Drummond—driving out of London in his car—a very nice Rolls, that new one of yours—bought, I think, since we last met. Your chauffeur would have been most uneasy when he missed it but for the note you've left him, saying you'll be away for three days." Peterson laughed gently as he stared at his victim.

"You must forgive me if I seem to gloat a little, won't you?" he continued. "I've got such a large score to settle with you, and I very much fear I shan't be in at the death. I have an engagement to dine with an American millionaire, whose wife is touched to the heart over the sufferings of the starving poor in Austria. And when the wives of millionaires are touched to the heart, my experience is that the husbands are generally touched to the pocket."

He laughed again even more gently and leaned across the table towards the man who sat motionless in the chair. He seemed to be striving to see some sign of fear in Drummond's eyes, some appeal for mercy. But if there was any expression at all it was only a faint mocking boredom, such as Drummond had been wont to infuriate him with during their first encounter a year before. Then he had expressed it in words and actions; now only his eyes were left to him, but it was there all the same. And after a while Peterson snarled at him viciously.

"No, I shan't be in at the death, Drummond, but I will explain to you the exact programme. You will be driven out of London in your own car, but when the final accident occurs you will be alone. It is a most excellent place for an accident, Drummond—most excellent. One or two have already taken place there, and the bodies are generally recovered some two or three days later—more or less unrecognizable. Then when the news comes out in the evening papers to-morrow I shall be able to tell the police the whole sad story. How you took compassion on an old clergyman and asked him to lunch, and then went out of London after your charming young wife—only to meet with this dreadful end. I think I'll even offer to take part in the funeral service. And yet—no, that is a pleasure I shall have to deny myself. Having done what I came over to do, Drummond, rather more expeditiously than I thought likely, I shall return to my starving children in Vienna. And, do you know what I came over to do, Drummond? I came over to smash the Black Gang—and I came over to kill you—though the latter could have waited."

Peterson's eyes were hard and merciless, but the expression of faint boredom still lingered in Drummond's. Only too well did he realize now that he had played straight into his enemy's hands, but he was a gambler through and through, and not by the quiver of an eyelid did he show what he felt. Right from the very start the dice had been loaded in Peterson's favour owing to that one astounding piece of luck in getting hold of Phyllis. It hadn't even been a fight—it had been a walk-over. And the cruel part of it was that it was not through any mistake of Drummond's. It was a fluke pure and simple—an astounding fluke—a fluke which had come off better than many a carefully-thought-out scheme. If it hadn't been for that he would never have come to Peterson's sitting-room at all; he would never have been doped; he wouldn't have been sitting helpless as a log while Peterson put down his cards one after the other in cold triumph.

"Yes, it could have waited, Captain Drummond—that second object of mine. I assure you that it was a great surprise to me when I realized who the leader of the Black Gang was—a great surprise and a great pleasure. To kill two birds so to speak, with one stone, saves trouble; to accomplish two objects in one accident is much more artistic. So the Black Gang loses its leader, the leader loses his life, and I regain my diamonds. Eminently satisfactory, my friend, eminently. And when your dear wife returns from the country—if she does, well, Captain Drummond, it will be a very astute member of Scotland Yard who will associate her little adventure with that benevolent old clergyman, the Reverend Theodosius Longmoor, who recently spent two or three days at the Ritz. Especially in view of your kindly telephone message to Mr.—what's his name?—Mr. Peter Darrell."

He glanced at his watch and rose to his feet.

"I fear that that is all the spiritual consolation that I can give you this evening, my dear fellow," he remarked benignly. "You will understand, I'm sure, that there are many calls on my time. Janet, my love"—he raised his voice—"our young friend is leaving us now. I feel sure you'd like to say good-bye to him."

She came into the room, walking a little slowly and for a while she stared in silence at Hugh. And it seemed to him that in her eyes there was a gleam of genuine pity. Once again he made a frantic effort to speak—to beg, beseech, and implore them not to hurt Phyllis—but it was useless. And then he saw her turn to Peterson.

"I suppose," she said regretfully, "that it is absolutely necessary."

"Absolutely," he answered curtly. "He knows too much, and he worries us too much."

She shrugged her shoulders and came over to Drummond.

"Well, good-bye, *mon ami*," she remarked gently. "I really am sorry that I shan't see you again. You are one of the few people that make this atrocious country bearable."

She patted him on his cheek, and again the feeling that he was dreaming came over Drummond. It couldn't be real—this monstrous nightmare. He would wake up in a minute and find Denny standing beside him, and he registered a vow that he would go to an indigestion specialist. And then he realized that the two men had come back into the room, and that it wasn't a dream, but hard, sober fact. The Italian was putting a hat on his head and wrapping the scarf round his neck while Peterson gave a series of curt instructions to the other man. And then he was being wheeled along the passage towards the lift, while the Reverend Theodosius Longmoor walked solicitously beside him, murmuring affectionately in his ear.

"Good-bye, my dear friend—good-bye," he remarked, after the chair had been wheeled into the lift. "It was good of you to come. Be careful, liftman, won't you?"

He waved a kindly hand, and the last vision Drummond had of him before the doors closed was of a benevolent old clergyman beaming at him solicitously from behind a pair of horn-rimmed spectacles.

And now came his only chance. Surely there would be someone who would recognize him below; surely the hall porter, who in the past had received many a tip from him, must realize who he was in spite of the hat pulled down over his eyes. But even that hope failed. The elderly party in the invalid's chair who had come half an hour ago was now going, and there was no reason why the hall porter should suspect anything. He gave the two men a hand lifting the chair into a big and very roomy limousine car which Drummond knew was certainly not his, and the next instant they were off.

He could see nothing—the hat was too far over his eyes. For a time he tried to follow where they were going by noting the turns, but he soon gave that up as hopeless. And then, after driving for about half an hour, the car stopped and the two men got out, leaving him alone. He could hear a lot of talking going on, but he didn't try to listen. He was resigned by this time—utterly indifferent; his only feeling was a mild curiosity as to what was going to happen next.

The voices came nearer, and he found himself being lifted out of the car. In doing so his hat was pulled back a little so that he could see, and the first thing he noticed was his own new Rolls-Royce. They couldn't have brought it to the Ritz, he reflected, where it might have been recognized—and an unwilling admiration for the master brain that had thought out every detail, and the wonderful organization that allowed of them being carried out, took hold of his mind.

The men wheeled him alongside his own car; then they lifted him out of his chair and deposited him on the back seat. Then the Italian and the other man who had been at the Ritz sat down one on each side of him, while a third man took the wheel.

"Look slippy, Bill," said the big man beside him. "A boat will be coming through about half-past nine."

A boat! What was that about a boat? Were they going to send him out to sea, then, and let him drown? If so, what was the object of getting his own car? The hat slipped forward again, but he guessed by some of the flaring lights he could dimly see that they were going through slums. Going eastward Essex way, or perhaps the south side of the river towards Woolwich. But after a time he gave it up; it was no good wondering—he'd know for certain soon enough. And now the speed was increasing as they left London behind them. The headlights were on, and Hugh judged that they were going about thirty-five miles an hour. And he also guessed that it was about forty-five minutes before they pulled up, and the engine and lights were switched off. The men beside him got out, and he promptly rolled over into a corner, where they left him lying.

"This is the place to wait," he heard the Italian say. "You go on, Franz, to the corner, and when it's ready flash your torch. You'll have to stand on the running-board, Bill, and steer till he's round the corner into the straight. Then jump off—no one will see you behind the headlights. I'm going back to Maybrick Tower."

And then he heard a sentence which drove him impotent with fury, and again set him struggling madly to move.

"The girl's there. We'll get orders about her in the morning."

There was silence for a while; then he heard Bill's voice.

"Let's get on with it. There's Franz signalling. We'll have to prop him up on the steering wheel somehow."

They pulled Drummond out of the back of the car, and put him in the driver's seat.

"Doesn't matter if he does fall over at the last moment. It will look as if he'd fainted, and make the accident more probable," said the Italian, and Bill grunted.

"Seems a crime," he muttered, "to smash up this peach of a car." He started the engine, and switched on the headlights; then he slipped her straight into third speed and started. He was on the running board beside the wheel, steering with one hand and holding on to Drummond with the other. And as they rounded the corner he straightened the car up and opened the throttle. Then he jumped off, and Drummond realized the game at last.

A river was in front—a river spanned by a bridge which swung open to let boats go through. And it was open now. He had a dim vision of a man waving wildly; he heard the crash as the car took the guarding gate, and then he saw the bonnet dip suddenly; there was a rending, scraping noise underneath him as the framework hit the edge; an appalling splash—and silence.

15

In which Hugh Drummond arrives at Maybrick Hall

Two things saved Drummond from what was practically certain death—the heavy coat he was wearing, and the fact that he rolled sideways clear of the steering wheel as soon as the man let go of him with his hand. Had he remained behind the wheel he must infallibly have gone to the bottom with the car, and at that point where the river narrowed to come through the piers of the bridge the water was over twenty feet deep. He had sufficient presence of mind to take a deep breath as the car shot downwards; then he felt the water close over his head. And if before his struggles to move had been fierce—now that the end seemed at hand they became desperate. The desire to get clear—to give one kick with his legs and come to the surface roused him to one superhuman effort. He felt as if the huge heave he gave with his legs against the floor-boards must send him flying to the top; afterwards he realized that this vast effort had been purely mental—the actual physical result had been practically negligible. But not quite, it had done something, and the coat did the rest.

With that one last supreme throw for life his mind had overcome the effects of the poison to the extent of forcing his legs to give one spasmodic little kick. He floated clear of the car, and slowly—how slowly only his bursting lungs could testify—the big coat brought him to the surface. For a moment or two he could do nothing save draw in deep gulps of air; then he realized that the danger was not yet past. For he couldn't shout, he could do nothing save float and drift, and the current had carried him clear of the bridge out of sight of those on top. And his mind was quite clear enough to realize that the coat which had saved him, once it became sodden would just as surely drown him.

He could see men with lanterns on the bridge; he could hear them shouting and talking. And then he saw a boat come back from the ship that had passed through just before he went over the edge in his car. Surely they'd pull down-stream to look for him, he thought in an agony of futile anger; surely they couldn't be such fools as to go on pulling about just by the bridge when it was obvious he wasn't there. But since they thought that he was at the bottom in his car, and blasphemous language was already being wafted at them by the skipper of the vessel for the useless delay, with a sinking heart Drummond saw the boat turn round and disappear up-stream into the darkness. Men with lanterns still stood on the bridge, but he was far beyond the range of their lights, and he was drifting further every minute. It was just a question of time now—and it couldn't be very long either. He could see that his legs had gone down well below the surface, and only the air that still remained in the buttoned-up part of his overcoat kept his head out and his shoulders near the top. And when that was gone—the end. He had done all he could; there was nothing for it now but to wait for the inevitable finish. And though he had been credibly informed that under such circumstances the whole of a man's life passes in rapid review before him, his sole and only thought was an intense desire to get his hands on Peterson again.

For a while he pictured the scene with a wealth of pleasant detail, until a sudden change in his immediate surroundings began to take place. At first he could not realize what had happened; then little by little it began to dawn on him what had occurred. Up to date the water in which he floated had seemed motionless to him; he had been drifting in it at exactly the same velocity as the current. And now, suddenly, he saw that the water was going past him. For a moment or two he failed to understand the significance of the fact; then wild hope surged up in his mind. For a time he stared fixedly at the bridge, and the hope became a certainty. He was not drifting any further from it; he was stationary; he was aground. He could feel nothing; he could see nothing—but the one stupendous fact remained that he was aground. Life took on another lease—anything might happen now. If only he could remain there till the morning they would see him from the bridge, and there seemed no reason why he shouldn't. The water still flowed sluggishly past him, broken with the faintest ripple close to his head. So he reasoned that it must be very shallow where he was, and being an incurable optimist, he resumed, with even fuller details, the next meeting with Peterson.

But not for long. Starting from his waist and spreading downwards to his feet and outwards through his shoulders to his hands there slowly began to creep the most agonising cramp. The torture was indescribable, and the sweat dripped off his forehead into his eyes. And gradually it dawned on him that the effects of the poison were wearing off. Sensation was returning to his limbs; even through his agony he could feel that he was resting against something under the water. Then he heard a strange noise, and realized that it was he himself groaning with the pain. The use of his voice had come back. He spoke a sentence aloud, and made certain.

And then Drummond deliberately decided on doing one of those things which Peterson had always failed to legislate for in the past. Ninety-nine men out of a hundred would have shouted themselves hoarse under such circumstances; not so Drummond. Had he done so a message would have reached Peterson in just so long as it took a trunk call to get through; the man called Franz was still assiduously helping the gate-keeper on the bridge. And the

Reverend Theodosius Longmoor and his little Janet would have vanished into the night, leaving no traces behind them.

Which all flashed through Drummond's mind, as the cramp took and racked him, and the impulse to shout grew stronger and stronger. Twice he opened his mouth to hail the men he could see not three hundred yards away—to give a cry that would bring a boat post-haste to his rescue; twice he stopped himself with the shout unuttered. A more powerful force was at work within him than mere pain—a cold, bitter resolve to get even with Carl Peterson. And it required no great effort of brain to see that that would be more easily done if Peterson believed he had succeeded. Moreover if he shouted there would be questions asked. The police would inevitably come into the matter, demanding to know why he adopted such peculiar forms of amusement as going into twenty feet of water in a perfectly good motor-car. And all that would mean delay, which was the last thing he wanted. He felt tolerably certain, that, for all his apparent confidence, Peterson was not going to stop one minute longer in the country than was absolutely necessary.

So he stayed where he was, in silence—and gradually the cramp passed away. He could turn his head now. and with eyes that had grown accustomed to the darkness he saw what had happened. On each side of him the river flowed past smoothly, and he realized that by a wonderful stroke of luck he had struck a small shoal. Had he missed it—had he floated by on either side—well, Peterson's plan would have succeeded.

"Following the extraordinary motor accident reported in our previous issue, we are now informed that the body of the unfortunate driver has been discovered some three miles from the scene of the tragedy. He was drowned, and had evidently been dead some hours."

Drummond smiled grimly to himself as he imagined the paragraphs in the papers. His nerves were far too hardened to let his narrow escape worry him for an instant, and he felt an unholy satisfaction in thinking of Peterson searching the early specials and the late extras for that little item of news.

"I'd hate you to be disappointed, my friend," he muttered to himself, "but you'll have to be content with the coat and hat. The body has doubtless drifted further on and will be recovered later."

He took off his hat, and let it drift away; he unbuttoned his overcoat and sent it after the hat. Then letting himself down into the deep water, he swam noiselessly towards the bank.

A little to his surprise he found that his legs and arms felt perfectly normal—a trifle stiff perhaps, but beyond that the effects of the poison seemed to have worn off completely. Beyond being very wet he appeared to have suffered no evil results at all, and after he'd done "knees up" on the bank for five minutes to restore his circulation he sat down to consider his plan of action.

First, Phyllis at Maybrick Hall. He must get at her somehow, and, even if he couldn't get her away, he must let her know that she would be all right. After that things must look after themselves; everything would depend on circumstances. Always provided that those circumstances led to the one great goal—Peterson. Once Phyllis was safe, everything was subservient to that.

A church clock near by began to toll the hour and Drummond counted the strokes. Eleven o'clock—not two hours since he had gone over the bridge—and it felt like six. So much the better; it gave him so many more hours of darkness, and he wanted darkness for his explorations at Maybrick Hall. And it suddenly dawned on him that he hadn't the faintest idea where the house was.

It might have deterred some men; it merely made Drummond laugh. If he didn't know, he'd find out—even if it became necessary to pull someone out of bed and ask. The first thing to do was to get back to the spot where the car had halted, and to do that he must go across country. Activity was diminishing on the bridge, but he could still see lanterns dancing about, and the sudden appearance of a very wet man might lead to awkward questions. So he struck off in the direction he judged to be right—moving with that strange, cat-like silence which was a never-ceasing source of wonderment even to those who knew him best.

No man ever heard Drummond coming, and very few ever saw him until it was too late, if he didn't intend that they should. And now, in utterly unknown country, with he knew not how many undesirable gentlemen about, he was taking no risks. Mercifully for him it was a dark night—just such a night in fact as he would have chosen, and as he passed like a huge shadow from tree to tree, only to vanish silently behind a hedge, and reappear two hundred yards further on, he began to feel that life was good. The joy of action was in his veins; he was going to get his hands on somebody soon, preferably the Italian or the man who called himself Franz. For Bill he had a sneaking regard; Bill at any rate could appreciate a good car when he saw one. The only trouble was that he was unarmed, and an unarmed man can't afford to stop and admire the view in a mix up. Not that the point deterred him for a moment, it only made him doubly cautious. He must see without being seen; he must act without being heard. Afterwards would be a different matter.

Suddenly he stiffened and crouched motionless behind a bush. He had heard voices and the sound of footsteps crunching on the gravel.

"No good waiting any more," said a man whom he recognized as Franz. "He's dead for a certainty, and they can't pull him out till to-morrow. Couldn't have gone better. He swayed right over just as the car took the gates, and the bridge-keeper saw it. Think he fainted——"

Their voices died away in the distance, and Drummond came out from behind the bush. He stepped forward cautiously and found himself confronted with a high wire fence. Through it he could see a road along which the two men must have been walking. And then through a gap in the trees he saw a light in the window of a house. So his first difficulty was solved. The man called Franz and his companion could have but one destination in all probability—Maybrick

Hall. And that must be the house he could see through the trees, while the road on the other side of the fence was the drive leading up to it.

He gave them half a minute or so; then he climbed through the fence. It was a fence with horizontal strands of thick wire, about a foot apart, and the top strand was two feet above Drummond's head. An expensive fence, he reflected; an unusual fence to put round any property of such a sort. An admirable fence for cattle in a corral because of its strength, but for a house and grounds—peculiar, to say the least. It was not a thing of beauty; it afforded no concealment, and it was perfectly simple to climb through. And because Drummond had been trained in the school which notices details, even apparently trivial ones, he stood for a moment or two staring at the fence, after he had clambered through. It was the expense of the thing more than anything else that puzzled him. It was new—that was obvious, and after a while, he proceeded to walk along it for a short way. And another peculiar thing struck him when he came to the first upright. It was an iron T-shaped post, and each strand of wire passed through a hole in the bottom part of the T. A perfectly simple and sound arrangement, and, but for one little point, just the type of upright one would have expected to find in such a fence. Round every hole was a small white collar, through which each strand of wire passed, so that the wires rested on the collars, and not on the holes of the iron upright. Truly a most remarkable fence, he reflected again—in fact, a thoroughly eccentric fence. But he got no further than that in his thoughts; the knowledge which would have supplied him with the one clue necessary to account for that fence's eccentricity of appearance was not his. The facts he could notice; the reason for the facts was beyond him. And after a further examination he shrugged his shoulders and gave it up. There were bigger things ahead of him than a mere question of fencing, and, keeping in the shadow of the shrubs which fringed each side of the drive, he crept silently towards the house.

It was a low rambling type of building covered as far as he could see with ivy and creepers. There were only two stories, and Hugh nodded his satisfaction. It made things simpler when outside work was more than likely. For a long time he stood in the shadow of a big rhododendron bush, carefully surveying every possible line of approach and flight, and it was while he was balancing up chances that he gradually became aware of a peculiar noise proceeding from the house. It sounded like the very faint hum of an aeroplane in the far distance, except that every two or three seconds there came a slight thud. It was quite regular, and during the four or five minutes whilst he stood there listening there was no variation in the monotonous rhythm. Thud, thud, thud—faint, but very distinct; and all the time the gentle whirring of some smooth-running, powerful engine.

The house was in darkness save for one room on the ground floor, from which the light was streaming. It was empty, and appeared to be an ordinary sitting-room. And, as a last resort, Hugh decided he would go in that way, if outside methods failed. But to start with he had no intention of entering the house; it struck him that the odds against him were unnecessarily large.

He retreated still further into the shadow, and then quite clear and distinct the hoot of an owl was heard in the silent garden. He knew that Phyllis would recognize the call if she heard it; he knew that she would give him some sign if she could. And so he stood and waited, eagerly watching the house for any sign of movement. But none came, and after a pause of half a minute he hooted again. Of course it was possible that she was in a room facing the other way, and he had already planned his line of advance round to the back of the house. And then, just as he was preparing to skirt round and investigate he saw the curtains of one of the upper rooms shake and open slightly. Very faintly he repeated the call, and to his joy he saw a head poked through between them. But he was taking no chances, and it was impossible to tell to whom the head belonged. It might be Phyllis, and on the other hand it might not. So once again he repeated the call, barely above his breath, and then he waited for some answer.

It came almost at once; his own name called very gently, and he hesitated no more. He was across the lawn in a flash and standing under her window, and once again he heard her voice tense with anxiety.

"Is that you, Hugh?"

"Yes, darling, it's me right enough," he whispered back. "But there's no time to talk now. I want you to jump on to the flower-bed. It's soft landing, and it won't hurt you."

"But I can't, old man," she said, with a little catch in her breath. "They've got me lashed up with a steel chain."

"They've got you lashed up with a steel chain," repeated Hugh stupidly. "The devil they have; the devil they have!"

And his voice was shaking a little with cold, concentrated fury.

"All right, kid," he went on after a moment "if you can't come to me I must come to you. We'll soon deal with that chain."

He glanced into the room underneath hers and saw that it looked like a drawing-room. The windows seemed easy to force if necessary, but he decided first of all to try the ivy outside. But it was useless for a man of his weight. Just at the bottom it supported him, but as soon as he started to climb it gave way at once. Twice he got up about six feet, twice he fell back again as the ivy broke away from the wall. And after the second attempt he looked up at the anxious face of his wife above.

"No go, darling," he muttered. "And I'm afraid of making too much noise. I'm going to try and force this window."

By a stroke of luck they had not taken his clasp-knife, and by a still greater stroke of luck he found that the catch on the window had been broken, and that it proved even easier to open than he had thought. He stepped back and looked up.

"I'm coming in, kid," he whispered. "Do you know where the stairs are?"

"Just about the middle of the house, old man. And listen. I can't quite reach the door to open it, but I've got my parasol and I can tap on it so that you'll know which it is."

"Right," he answered. "Keep your tail up."

The next moment he had vanished into the drawing-room. And now he noticed that that strange noise which he had heard while standing on the lawn was much louder. As he cautiously opened the door and peered into the passage the very faint hum became a steady drone, while with each successive thud the floorboards shook a little.

The passage was in darkness, though light was shining from under some of the doors. And as he crept along in search of the stairs he heard voices proceeding from one of the rooms he passed. Evidently a fairly populous household, it struck him, as he tested the bottom stair with his weight to see if it creaked. But the staircase was old and solid, and the stair carpet was thick, and at the moment Hugh was not disposed to linger. Afterwards the house seemed to promise a fairly fruitful field for investigation; at present Phyllis was all that mattered. So he vanished upwards with the uncanny certainty of all his movements at night, and a moment later he was standing on the landing above.

It was a long, straight corridor, a replica of the one below, and he turned in the direction in which he knew her room must lie. And he had only taken a couple of steps when he stopped abruptly, peering ahead with eyes that strove to pierce the darkness. For it seemed to him that there was something in the passage—something darker than its surroundings. He pressed against the wall absolutely motionless, and as he stood there with every sense alert, and his arms hanging loosely forward ready for any emergency, he heard a tapping on one of the doors just ahead of him. It was Phyllis signalling with her parasol as she had said, and he took a step forward. And at that moment something sprang out of the darkness, and he found himself fighting for his life.

For a second or two he was at a disadvantage, so completely had he been taken by surprise; then the old habits returned. And not a moment too soon; he was up against an antagonist who was worthy of him. Two hands like iron hooks were round his neck, and the man who gets that grip first wins more often than not. His own hands shot out into the darkness, and then for the first time in his life he felt a stab of fear. For he couldn't reach the other man: long though his arms were, the other man's were far longer, and as his hands went along them he could feel the muscles standing out like steel bars. He made one supreme effort to force through to his opponent's throat and it failed; with his superior reach he could keep his distance. Already Drummond's head was beginning to feel like bursting with the awful pressure round his throat, and he knew he must do something at once or lose. And just in time he remembered his clasp-knife. It went against his grain to use it; never before had he fought an unarmed man with a weapon—and as far as he could tell this man was unarmed. But it had to be done and done quickly.

With all his force he stabbed sideways at the man's left arm. He heard a snarl of pain, and the grip of one of the hands round his throat relaxed. And now the one urgent thing was to prevent him shouting for help. Like a flash Drummond was on him, one hand on his mouth and the other gripping his throat with the grip he had learned from Osaki the Jap in days gone by, and had never forgotten. And because he was fighting to kill now he wasted no time. The grip tightened; there was a dreadful worrying noise as the man bit into his thumb—then it was over. The man slipped downwards on to the floor, and Drummond stood drawing in great mouthfuls of air.

But he knew there was no time to lose. Though they had fought in silence, and he could still hear the monotonous thud and the beat of the engine, at any moment someone might come upstairs. And to be found with a dead man at one's feet in a strange house is not the best way of securing a hospitable welcome. What to do with the body—that was the first insistent point. There was no time for intricate schemes; it was a question of taking risks and chancing it. So for a moment or two he listened at the door of the room opposite that on which he had heard Phyllis tapping, and from which the man had sprung at him—then he gently opened it. It was a bedroom and empty, and without further hesitation he dragged his late opponent in, and left him lying on the floor. By the dim light from the uncurtained window he could see that the man was almost deformed, so enormous was the length of his arms. They must have been six inches longer than those of an average man, and were almost as powerful as his own. And as he saw the snarling, ferocious face upturned to his, he uttered a little prayer of thanksgiving for the presence of his clasp-knife. It had been altogether too near a thing for his liking.

He closed the door and stepped across the passage, and the next moment Phyllis was in his arms.

"I thought you were never coming, old man," she whispered. "I was afraid the brutes had caught you."

"I had a slight difference of opinion with a warrior outside your door," said Hugh, grinning. "Quite like old times."

"But, my dear," she said, with sudden anxiety in her voice, "you're sopping wet."

"Much water has flowed under the bridge, my angel child, since I last saw you, and I've flowed with it." He kissed her on the right side of her mouth, then on the left for symmetry, and finally in the middle for luck. Then he grew serious. "No time for hot air now, old thing; let's have a look at this jolly old chain effect of yours. Once we're out of here, you shall tell me everything and I'll eat several pounds of mud for having been such an unmitigated idiot as to let these swine get hold of you."

He was examining the steel chain as he spoke, and gradually his face grew grave. He didn't seem to have gained much after all by breaking in; Phyllis was just as much a prisoner as ever. The chain, which was about six feet long, was fastened at one end to a big staple in the wall and at the other end to a bracelet which encircled his wife's right wrist. And the bracelet could only be opened with a key. Any idea of breaking the chain or pulling out the staple was so preposterous as not to be worth even a moment's thought; so everything depended on the bracelet. And when he came to examine it more carefully he found that it had a Yale lock.

He sat down on the edge of the bed, and she watched him anxiously.

"Can't you get it undone, boy?" she whispered.

"Not if I stopped here till next Christmas, darling," he answered heavily.

"Well, get out of the window and go for the police," she implored.

"My dear," he said, still more heavily, "I had, as I told you, a little difference of opinion with the gentleman outside the door—and he's very dead." She caught her breath sharply. "A nasty man with long arms who attacked me. It might be all right, of course—but I somehow feel that this matter is beyond the local constable, even if I could find him. You see, I don't even know where we are." He checked the exclamation of surprise that rose to her lips. "I'll explain after, darling; let's think of this now. If only I could get the key; if only I knew where it was, even."

"A foreigner came in about an hour ago," answered his wife. "He had it then. And he said he'd come again to-night."

"He did, did he?" said Hugh slowly. "I wonder if it's my friend the Italian. Anyway, kid, it's the only chance. Did he come alone last time?"

"Yes: I don't think there was anyone with him. I'm sure there wasn't."

"Then we must chance it," said Hugh. "Say something; get him into the room and then leave him to me. And if for any reason he doesn't come I'll have to leave you here and raise the gang."

"Wouldn't it be safer, boy, to do that now?" she said imploringly. "Suppose anything happened to you."

"Anything further that happens to me to-night, old thing," he remarked grimly, "will be as flat as a squashed pancake compared to what's happened already."

And then because she saw his mind was made up, and she knew the futility of arguing under those conditions, she sat on the bed beside him to wait. For a while they sat in silence listening to the monotonous thudding noise which went ceaselessly on; then because he wanted to distract her mind he made her tell him what had happened to her. And in disjointed whispers, with his arm round her waist, she pieced together the gaps in the story. How the man had come about the electric light, and then had offered to fetch her a taxi, he knew already from Denny. She had got in, never suspecting anything, and told him to drive to the Ritz—and almost at once she had begun to feel faint. Still she suspected nothing, until she tried to open one of the windows. But it wouldn't open, and the last thing she remembered before she actually fainted was tapping on the glass to try to draw the driver's attention. Then when she came to, she found to her horror that she was not alone. A man was in the car with her, and they were out of London in the country. Both windows were wide open, and she asked him furiously what he was doing in her car. He smiled, and remarked that so far he was not aware he had sold it, but he was always open to an offer. And it was then that she realized for the first time exactly what had happened.

The man told her quite frankly that she hadn't fainted at all, but had been rendered unconscious by a discharge of gas down the speaking-tube; that acting under orders he was taking her to a house in the country where she would have to remain for how long he was unable to say, and further if she made a sound or gave any trouble he would gag her on the spot.

Hugh's arm tightened round her waist, and he cursed fluently under his breath.

"And what happened when you got here, darling?" he asked as she paused.

"They brought me straight up here, and tied me up," she answered. "They haven't hurt me—and they've given me food, but I've been terrified—simply terrified—as to what they were going to do next." She clung to him, and he kissed her reassuringly. "There's a man below with red hair and a straggling beard, who came and stared at me in the most horrible way. He was in his shirt sleeves and his arms were all covered with chemical stains."

"Did he touch you?" asked Hugh grimly.

"No—he just looked horrible," she said, with a shudder. "And then he repeated the other man's threat—the one who had been in the car—that if I shouted or made any fuss he'd lash me up and gag me. He spoke in a sort of broken English—and his voice never seemed to rise above a whisper."

She was trembling now, and Hugh made a mental note of another gentleman on whom he proposed to lay hands in the near future. Red hair and a straggling beard should not prove hard to recognize.

He glanced at the watch on Phyllis's wrist, and saw that it was very nearly one o'clock. The noise of the engine was still going monotonously on; except for that the house seemed absolutely silent. And he began to wonder how long it would be wise to continue the vigil. Supposing no one did come; supposing somebody came who hadn't got the key; supposing two or three of them came at the same time. Would it be better, even now, to drop through the window—and try to find a telephone or the police? If only he knew where he was; it might take him hours to find either at that time of night. And his whole being revolted at the idea of leaving Phyllis absolutely defenceless in such a house.

He rose and paced softly up and down the room trying to think what was the best thing to do. It was a maddening circle whichever way he looked at it, and his fists clenched and unclenched as he tried to make up his mind. To go or to wait; to go at once or to stop in the hope that one man would come up and have the key on him. Common sense suggested the first course; something far more powerful than common sense prompted the other. He could not and would not leave Phyllis alone, and so he decided on a compromise. If when daylight came no one had been up to the room, he would go; but he would wait until then. She'd feel safer once the night was over, and in the dawn he would be able to find his way outside more easily.

And he was just going to tell Phyllis what he had decided, when he heard a sound that killed the words on his lips. A door had opened below, and men's voices came floating up the stairs.

"Lie down, darling," he breathed in her ear, "and pretend to be asleep."

Without a word she did as he told her, while Hugh tiptoed over towards the door. There were steps coming up the stairs, and he flattened himself against the wall—waiting. The period of indecision was passed; unless he was very much mistaken the time of action had arrived. How it would pan out—whether luck would be in, or whether luck would fail was on the lap of the gods. All he could do was to hit hard and if necessary hit often, and a tingle of pure joy spread over him. Even Phyllis was almost forgotten at the moment; he had room in his mind for one thought only—the man whose steps he could hear coming along the passage.

There was only one of them, he noted with a sigh of relief—but for all that silence would be essential. It would take time to find the key; it would take even longer to get Phyllis free and out of the house. So there must be no risk of an alarm whatever happened.

The steps paused outside the door, and he heard a muttered ejaculation in Italian. It was his own particular friend of the motor right enough, and he grinned gently to himself. Apparently he was concerned over something, and it suddenly dawned on Drummond that it was the absence from duty of the long-armed bird that was causing the surprise. In the excitement of the moment he had forgotten all about him, and for one awful second his heart stood still. Suppose the Italian discovered the body before he entered the room, then the game was up with a vengeance. Once the alarm was given he'd have to run the gauntlet of the whole crowd over ground he didn't know.

But his fears were groundless; the non-discovery of the watcher by the door took the Italian the other way. His first thought was to make sure that the girl was safe, and he flung open the door and came in. He gave a grunt of satisfaction as he saw her lying on the bed; then like a spitting cat he swung round as he felt Drummond's hand on his shoulder.

"*È pericoloso spargersi*," muttered Hugh pleasantly, recalling the only Italian words he knew.

"*Dio mio!*" stammered the other, with trembling lips. Like most southerners he was superstitious, and to be told it was dangerous to lean out of the window by a man whom he knew to be drowned was too much for him. It was a ghost; it could be nothing else, and his knees suddenly felt strangely weak.

"You didn't know I was a linguist, did you?" continued Hugh, still more pleasantly; and with every ounce of weight in his body behind the blow, he hit the Italian on the point of the jaw. Without a sound the man crumpled up and pitched on his face.

And now there was not a moment to be lost. At any moment one of his pals might come upstairs, and everything depended on speed and finding the key. Hugh shut the door and locked it; then feverishly he started to search through the Italian's pockets. Everything up to date had panned out so wonderfully that he refused to believe that luck was going to fail him now, and sure enough he discovered the bunch in one of the unconscious man's waistcoat pockets. There were four of them, and the second he tried was the right one. Phyllis was free, and he heard her give a little sob of pure excitement.

"You perfectly wonderful boy!" she whispered, and Hugh grinned.

"We'll hurl floral decorations afterwards, my angel," he remarked. "Just at the moment it seems a pity not to replace you with someone."

He heaved the Italian on the bed, and snapped the steel bracelet on to his arm. Then he slipped the keys into his own pocket, and crossed to the window. The engine was still humming gently; the thudding noise was still going on; nothing seemed in any way different. No light came from the room below them, everything had worked better than he had dared to hope. He had only to lower Phyllis out of the window, and let her drop on to the flower-bed and then follow himself. After that it was easy.

"Come along, darling," he said urgently. "I'm going to lower you out first—then I'll follow. And once we're down, you've got to trice up your skirts and run like a stag across the lawn till we're under cover of those bushes. We aren't quite out of the wood yet."

They were not indeed. It was just as Phyllis let go, and he saw her pick herself up and dart across the lawn, that he heard a terrific uproar in the house below, and several men came pounding up the stairs. There were excited voices in the passage outside, and for a moment he hesitated, wondering what on earth had caused the sudden alarm. Then realizing that this was no time for guessing acrostics, he vaulted over the window-sill himself, and lowered himself to the full extent of his arms. Then he, too, let go and dropped on the flower bed below. And it was as he was picking himself up, preparatory to following Phyllis—whom he could see faintly across the lawn waiting for him, that he heard someone in the house shout an order in a hoarse voice.

"Switch on the power at once, you damned fool; switch it on at once!"

16

In which things happen at Maybrick Hall

Had the Italian come up five minutes sooner—a minute even—all would have been well. As it was, at the very moment when Drummond's crashing blow took him on the point of the jaw with mathematical precision, another mathematical law began to operate elsewhere—the law of gravity. Something fell from a ceiling on to a table in the room below that ceiling, even as in days gone by an apple descended into the eye of the discoverer of that law.

The two men seated in the room below the ceiling in question failed to notice it at first. They were not interested in mathematics but they were interested in their conversation. One was the red-haired man of whom Phyllis had spoken; the other was a nondescript type of individual who looked like an ordinary middle-class professional man.

"Our organization has, of course, grown immensely," he was saying. "Our Socialist Sunday Schools, as you may know, were started twenty-five years ago. A very small beginning, my friend, but the result now would stagger you. And wishy-washy stuff was taught to start with too; now I think even you would be satisfied."

Something splashed on the table beside him, but he took no notice.

"Blasphemy, of course—or rather what the bourgeois call blasphemy—is instilled at once. We teach them to fear no God; we drive into them each week that the so-called God is merely a weapon of the capitalist class to keep them quiet, and that if it had not that effect they would see what a machine-gun could do. And, Yulowski, it is having its effect.

"Get at the children has always been my motto—for they are the next generation. They can be moulded like plastic clay; their parents, so often, are set in a groove. We preach class hatred—and nothing but class hatred. We give them songs to sing—songs with a real catchy tune. There's one very good one in which the chorus goes:

"'Come, workers, sing a rebel song, a song of love and hate,
Of love unto the lowly and of hatred to the great.'"

He paused to let the full effect of the sublime stanza sink in, and again something splashed on to the table.

Yulowski nodded his head indifferently.

"I admit its value, my friend," he remarked in a curious husky whisper. "And in your country I suppose you must go slowly. I fear my inclinations lead towards something more rapid and—er—drastic. Sooner or later the bourgeois must be exterminated all the world over. On that we are agreed. Why not make it sooner as we did in Russia? The best treatment for any of the capitalist class is a bayonet in the stomach and a rifle butt on the head."

He smiled reminiscently, a thin, cruel smile, and once again there came an unheeded splash.

"I have heard it said," remarked the other man, with the faintest hesitation, "that you yourself were responsible in Russia for a good many of them."

The smile grew more pronounced and cruel.

"It was I, my friend, who battered out the brains of two members of the Arch Tyrant's family. Yes, I—I who sit here." His voice rose to a sort of throaty shout and his eyes gleamed. "You can guess who I mean, can't you?"

"Two girls," muttered the other, recoiling a little in spite of himself.

"Two——" The foul epithet went unuttered; Yulowski was staring fascinated at the table. "Holy Mother! what's that?"

His companion swung round, and every vestige of colour left his face. On the table was a big red pool, and even as he watched it there came another splash and a big drop fell into it.

"Blood!" he stammered, and his lips were shaking. "It's blood." And then he heard the Russian's voice, low and tense.

"Look at the ceiling, man; look at the ceiling."

He stared upwards and gave a little cry of horror. Slowly spreading over the white plaster was a great crimson stain, whilst from a crack in the middle the steady drip fell on to the table.

It was Yulowski who recovered himself first; he was more used to such sights than his companion.

"There's been murder done," he shouted hoarsely, and dashed out of the room. Doors were flung open, and half a dozen men rushed up the stairs after him. There was no doubt which the room was, and headed by Yulowski they crowded in—only to stop and stare at what lay on the floor.

"It's the Greek," muttered one of them. "He was guarding the girl. And someone has severed the main artery in his arm."

With one accord they dashed across the passage to the room where Phyllis had been. In a second the door was broken in, and they saw the unconscious Italian lying on the bed.

"The Black Gang," muttered someone fearfully, and Yulowski cursed him for a cowardly swine. And it was his hoarse voice that Drummond heard shouting for the power to be switched on, as he turned and darted across the lawn.

Completely ignorant of what had taken place, he was just as ignorant of what was meant by switching on the power. His one thought now was to get away with Phyllis. A start meant everything, and at the best he couldn't hope for a long one. With his arm through hers he urged her forward, while behind him he heard a confused shouting which gradually died away under the peremptory orders of someone who seemed to be in command. And almost subconsciously he noticed that the thudding noise had ceased; only the faint humming of the engine broke the silence.

Suddenly in front of him he saw the fence which had caused him to wonder earlier in the evening. It was just the same in this part as it had been in the other, but he wasn't concerned with speculations about it now. The only thing he was thankful for was that it was easy to get through.

He was not five feet from it, when it happened—the amazing and at the moment inexplicable thing. For months after he used to wake in the night and lie sweating with horror at the nearness of the escape. For it would have been Phyllis who would have gone through first; it would have been Phyllis, who—But it did happen—just in time.

He saw a dark shape dart across the open towards the fence, an animal carrying something in its mouth. It reached the fence, and the next instant it bounded an incredible height in the air, only to fall backwards on to the ground and lie motionless almost at Drummond's feet. It was so utterly unexpected that he paused instinctively and stared at it. It was a fox, and the fowl it had been carrying lay a yard away. It lay there rigid and motionless, and completely bewildered he bent and touched it, only to draw back his hand as if he'd been stung. A sharp stabbing pain shot up his arm, as if he'd had an electric shock—and suddenly he understood, and with a cry of fear he dragged Phyllis back just in time.

The brain moves rapidly at times; the inherent connection of things takes place in a flash. And the words he had used to the Italian, *È pericoloso sporgersi*, took him back to Switzerland, where the phrase is written on every railway carriage. And in Switzerland, you may see those heavy steel pylons with curved, pointed hooks to prevent people climbing up, and red bands painted with the words *Danger de mort*. Live wires there are at the top, carried on insulators—even as the fence wires were carried through insulators in the uprights.

Danger de mort. And the fox had been electrocuted. That was what the man had meant by shouting for the power to be switched on. And as he stood there still clutching Phyllis's arm, and shaken for the moment out of his usual calm, there came from the direction of the house, the deep-throated baying of a big hound.

"What is it, Hugh?" said Phyllis in an agonized whisper.

With terrified eyes she was staring at the body of the fox, stiff and rigid in death, and with its jaws parted in a hideous snarl. And again there came from the direction of the house a deep-throated bay.

Then suddenly she realized that her husband was speaking—quietly, insistently. Only too well did he know the danger: only too well did he know that never before in his life had the situation been so tight. But no sign of it showed on his face: not a trace of indecision appeared in his voice. The position was desperate, the remedy must be desperate, too.

"We can't climb through the fence, dear," he was saying calmly. "You see they've switched an electric current through the wires, and if you touch one you'll be electrocuted. Also they seem to have turned an unpleasant little animal into the garden, so we can't stay here. At least—you can't. So I'm going to throw you over the top."

In an agony of fear she clung to him for a moment: then as she saw his quiet, set face she pulled herself together and smiled. There was no time for argument now: there was no time for anything except instant action. And being a thoroughbred, she was not going to hinder him by any weakness on her part. Of fear for herself she felt no trace: her faith and trust in her husband was absolute. And so she stood there silently waiting while he measured height and distance with his eye.

Of his ability to get her over he felt no doubt: but when a mistake means death to the woman he loves a man does not take risks.

"Come, dear," he said after a moment's pause. "Put your knees close up to your chin, and try and keep like a ball until you feel yourself falling."

She doubled herself up and he picked her up. One hand held both her feet—the other gripped the waistband at the back of her skirt. Once he lifted her above his head to the full extent of his arms to free his muscles: then he took a little run and threw her up and forward with all his strength. And she cleared the top strand by two feet.

She landed unhurt in some bushes, and when she had scrambled to her feet she realized he was speaking again—imperatively, urgently.

"Get the gang, darling: somehow or other get the gang. I'll try and get you a good start. But—hurry."

The next instant he had disappeared into the undergrowth, and only just in time. A huge hound running mute had dashed into the clearing where a second or two before they had been standing, and was cautiously approaching the dead fox. She stared at it fascinated, and then with a little cry of terror she pulled herself together and ran. She had forgotten the fence that was between them: for the moment she had forgotten everything except this huge brute that looked the size of a calf. And the hound, seeing the flutter of her dress, forgot things too. A dead fox could wait, a living human was better fun by far. He bounded forward: gave one agonized roar as he hit the fence, and turning a complete somersault lay still. And as Phyllis stumbled blindly on, she suddenly heard Hugh's cheerful voice from the darkness behind her, apparently addressing the world at large.

"Roll up! roll up! roll up! one fox: one Pomeranian: one fowl. No charge for admittance. Visitors are requested not to touch the exhibits."

And then the loud and clear hoot of an owl thrice repeated. It was a message for her, she knew—not a senseless piece of bravado: a message to tell her that he was all right. But the call at the end was the urgent call of the gang, and though he was safe at the moment she knew there was no time to be lost. And, with a little prayer that she would choose the right direction, she broke into the steady run of the girl who beagles when she goes beagling, and doesn't sit on the top of a hill and watch. Hugh had never let her down yet: it was her turn now.

To what extent it was her turn, perhaps it was as well that she did not realize. Even Drummond, hidden in the undergrowth just by the clearing where lay the body of the hound, was ignorant of the nature of the odds against him. He had not the slightest idea how many men there were in the house—and while it remained dark he didn't much care. In the dark he felt confident of dealing with any number, or at any rate of eluding them. It was the thing of all others that his soul loved—that grim fighting at night, when a man looks like the trunk of a tree, and the trunk of a tree looks like a man. It was in that that he was unequalled—superb: and the inmates of Maybrick Hall would have been well advised to have stayed their hands till the light came. Then the position, in military parlance, could have been taken without loss. An unarmed man is helpless when he can be seen.

But since the inmates were ignorant of what they were up against, they somewhat foolishly decided on instant action. They came streaming across in a body in the track of the dead hound, and by so doing they played straight into the hands of the man who crouched in the shadows close by them. He listened for one moment to the babel of tongues of every nationality, and decided that a little more English might adjust the average. So without a sound he faded away from his hiding-place, and emerged from the undergrowth ten yards nearer the house. Then with his collar turned up, and his shoulders hunched together, he joined the group. And a man-eating tiger in their midst would have been a safer addition to their party.

Certain it is that the next quarter of an hour proved a period of such terror for the inmates of Maybrick Hall that at the end of that time they reassembled at the house and flatly refused to budge, despite the threats and curses of the red-headed Russian. For Drummond had heard the original orders—to form a line of beaters and shoot on sight—and had smiled gently to himself in the darkness. There is always an element of humour in stalking the stalkers, and when the line formed up at intervals of two or three yards the quarry was behind it. Moreover the quarry was angry, with the cold, steady rage of a powerful man who realizes exactly what he is up against. Shoot on sight was the order, and Drummond accepted the terms.

Slowly the line of shadowy men moved forward through the undergrowth, and creeping behind them came the man they were out to kill. And gradually he edged nearer and nearer to the wire fence, until he was following the outside man of the line. He saw him pause for a moment peering round a bush, with his revolver ready in his hand. And then the terror started. The beater next to the victim had a fleeting vision of a huge black object springing through the darkness: a muttered curse and a gurgle—and a dreadful strangled scream. And the outside beater was no more. He had been hurled against the live-wire fence as if he was a child—-and the exhibits had been increased by one.

With a hoarse cry of fear the man who had been next him turned and ran towards the house, only to find himself seized from behind with a grip of iron. It was Franz, and as he stared into the face of the man whom he knew to be drowned he gave a squawk like a trapped rabbit. But there was nothing ghostly about the hands round his neck, and as he felt himself being rushed towards the fence of death he began to struggle furiously. But Drummond was mad at the moment, and though Franz was a powerful man he might have saved himself the trouble. A terrific blow hit him on the face, and with a grunt he fell back against the fence. The exhibits were increased by two, and through the darkness rang a cheerful laugh, followed by the hooting of an owl.

And now the line was broken, and men were crashing about in all directions shouting hoarsely. Experts of the Red Terror they might be—butcherers of women and children whose sole fault lay in the fact that they washed: that night they found themselves up against a terror far worse than even their victims had ever experienced. For they, poor wretches, knew what was coming: the men who ran shouting through the undergrowth did not. Here, there, and everywhere they heard the hooting of an owl: they formed into bunches of twos and threes for protection, they blazed away with compressed-air revolvers at harmless rhododendron bushes, and sometimes at their own pals. And every now and then a great black figure would leap silently out of the darkness on to some straggler: there would be a bellow of fear and pain followed by an ominous silence, which was broken a second or two later by the hooting of an owl twenty yards away.

Occasionally they saw him—a dim, fleeting shadow, and once four of them fired at him simultaneously. But luck was with him, and though two holes were drilled in his coat Drummond was not hit himself. His quiet laugh came suddenly from behind them, and even as they swung round cursing, one of them collapsed choking with a bullet through his chest. It was the first time he had used his first victim's revolver, but the target was too tempting to be let off. And at last they could stand it no longer. They had no idea how many men they were up against, and a complete panic set in. With one accord they rushed for the house, and a mocking peal of laughter followed them as they ran. For Drummond had gambled on that, and he had won. In the position of knowing that every man was his enemy, he had been at an advantage over the others, who were never sure who was a friend. For a while he listened to the flood of lurid blasphemy which came from the open windows of the room into which they had crowded: then he dodged along the bushes and looked in. For a moment he was sorely tempted to fire: in fact he went so far as to draw a bead on the red-headed Russian, who was gesticulating furiously. Then his hand dropped to his side: shooting into the brown was not his idea of the game. And at the same moment, the lights were switched off in the room: it had evidently struck someone inside that the position was a trifle insecure. The talking ceased abruptly, and with a faint grin on his face Drummond swung round and vanished into the deepest part of the undergrowth. It was necessary to do some thinking.

He had got the start he wanted for Phyllis, which was all to the good, but he was as far as ever himself from getting out. There was still the fence to be negotiated if he was to escape, and common sense told him that there wasn't the remotest chance of the current having been switched off. And incidentally, it didn't much matter whether it had been or not, since the only way of finding out for certain was to touch one of the wires—a thing he had not the faintest intention of doing. He could still hear the steady thrumming of the engine, and so the fence was out of the question.

Delving into memories of the past, when he had sat at the feet of the stinks master at his school, he tried to remember some of the gems of wisdom, anent electricity, which had fallen from his lips. But since his sole occupation during such lectures had been the surreptitious manufacture of sulphuretted hydrogen from a retort concealed below his desk, he finally gave up the attempt in despair. One thing was certain: the fence must be continuous. From knowledge gained from the sparking plugs of his car, he knew that a break in the circuit was fatal. Therefore there could be no break in the fence which encircled the house. And if that was so—how about the drive? How did the drive pass through the fence? There must be a break there, or something capable of forming a break. A motor-car will not go over an eight-foot fence, and he had seen the wheel tracks of a car quite clearly on the drive earlier in the evening.

Yes—he would try the gate. It was imperative to get away, and that as soon as possible. When dawn came, and the first faint streaks were already beginning to show in the east, he realized that he would be at a hopeless disadvantage. Moreover the absolute silence which now reigned after the turmoil and shouting of the last few minutes struck him as ominous. And Drummond was far too clever a man to under-rate his opponents. The panic had been but a temporary affair; and the panic was now over.

He began to thread his way swiftly and silently in the direction of the drive. Not for a second did he relax his caution, though he felt tolerably certain that all his opponents were still inside the house. Only too well did he know that the greatest danger often lies when things seems safest. But he reached the edge of the drive without incident, and started to skirt along it away from the house. At last he saw the gate, and turned deeper into the undergrowth. He wanted to examine it at leisure, before making up his mind as to what he would do. As far as he could see from the outline he could make out against the road, it was an ordinary heavy wooden gate, such as may be seen frequently at the entrance to small country houses.

A tiny lodge lay on one side: the usual uncared for undergrowth on the other. He could see the wire fence coming to the gatepost on each side; he could see that the strands were bunched together at the gate as telegraph wires are bunched when they pass underneath a bridge on a railway line. And it was while he was cogitating on the matter that he saw a man approaching from the other side. He came up to the gate, climbed over it with the utmost nonchalance, and turned into the little lodge. And Hugh noticed that as he climbed he was careful to avoid the second horizontal from the ground. At last it seemed to him that everything was clear. Contact was made through the latch; the current passed along the wires which were laid on the top of the second horizontal from the ground, and thence to the continuation of the fence on the other side. Anyway, whatever the electrical device, if this man could climb the gate in safety—so could he. There was a risk—a grave risk. It meant going out into the open; it meant exposing himself for a considerable period. But every moment he delayed the light grew better, and the risk became worse. And it was either that or waiting in the garden till daylight made his escape impossible. And still he hung back.

Men who knew Hugh Drummond well often said that he had a strange sixth sense which enabled him to anticipate danger, when to others with him everything seemed perfectly safe. Well-nigh fantastic stories were told of him by men who had accompanied him on those unofficial patrols he had carried out in No Man's Land whenever his battalion was in the line, and frequently when it wasn't. And as he stood there motionless as a statue, with only the ceaseless movement of his eyes to show his strained attention, that sixth sense of his warned him, and continued warning him insistently. There was danger: he felt it, he knew it—though where it lay he couldn't tell.

And then suddenly he again saw a man approaching from the other side—a man who climbed the gate with the utmost nonchalance and turned into the little lodge. He too carefully avoided the second horizontal from the ground, but Drummond was not paying any attention to the gate now. Once again his sixth sense had saved him, for it was the same man who had climbed over the first time. And why should a man adopt such a peculiar form of amusement, unless he was deliberately acting as a decoy? He had disappeared into the lodge, only to leave it again by a back entrance—and in an instant the whole thing was clear. They had gambled on his going to the gate: they had gambled on his having a dart for it when he saw the gate was safe to climb. And he smiled grimly when he realized how nearly they had won their bet.

Suddenly his eyes riveted themselves on the little hedge in front of the lodge. Something had stirred there: a twig had snapped. And the smile grew more grim as he stared at the shadow. Up to date it was the gate that had occupied his attention—now he saw that the hedge was alive with men. And after a while he began to shake gently with laughter. The idea of the perspiring sportsman trotting in and out of the back door, to show off his particular line in gates, while a grim bunch of bandits lay on their stomachs in the dew, hoping for the best, appealed to his sense of humour. For the moment the fact that he was now hopelessly trapped did not trouble him: his whole soul went out to the painstaking gate-hopper. If only he would do it again—that was his one prayer. And sure enough about five minutes later he hove in sight again, stepping merrily and brightly along the road.

His nonchalance was superb: he even hummed gently to show his complete disdain for gates in general and this one in particular. And then Drummond plugged him through the leg. He felt that it would have been a crime to end the career of such a bright disposition: so he plugged him through the fleshy part of the leg. And the man's howl of pain and Drummond's raucous bellow of laughter broke the silence simultaneously.

Not the least merry interlude, he reflected, in an evening devoted to fun and games, as he took cover rapidly behind a big tree. For bullets were whistling through the undergrowth in all directions, as the men who had been lying under cover of the hedge rose and let fly. And then quite abruptly the shooting died away, and Drummond became aware that a car was approaching. The headlights were throwing fantastic shadows through the bushes, and outlined against the glare he could see the figures of his opponents. Now was his chance, and with the quickness of the born soldier he acted on it. If the car was to come in they must open the gate; and since nothing blinds anyone so completely as the dazzle of strong headlights, he might be able to slip out unseen, just after the car had passed through. He skirted rapidly to one side out of the direct beam: then he made his way towards the lodge, keeping well out on the flank. And from a concealed position under cover of the little house he awaited developments.

The man he had shot through the leg was unceremoniously bundled on to the grass beside the drive, whilst another man climbed the gate and went up to the car, which had come to a standstill ten yards or so away. Drummond heard the sound of a window being lowered, and an excited conversation; then the man who had approached the car stepped back again into the glare of the headlights.

"Open the gate," he said curtly, and there was a sardonic grin on his face.

And now Drummond was waiting tensely. If he was to bring it off it would be a matter of seconds and half-seconds. Little by little he edged nearer to the drive, as a man with what appeared to be a huge glove on his hand approached the gate. There was a bright flash as he pressed down the catch and the circuit was broken, and at the same moment the headlights on the car went out, while an inside light was switched on.

And Drummond stopped dead—frozen in his tracks. The car was moving forward slowly, and he could see the people inside clearly. One was Count Zadowa—*alias* Mr. Atkinson; one was the Reverend Theodosius Longmoor. But the other—and it was the third person on whom his eyes were fixed with a hopeless feeling of impotent rage—the other was Phyllis herself. The two men were holding her in front of them, so that to fire was an impossibility, and Peterson was smiling out of the window with the utmost benevolence. Then they were past him, and he watched the red tail-lamp disappearing up the drive, while the gate was shut behind them. Another flashing spark stabbed the darkness: the circuit was complete again. And with a feeling of sick, helpless fury, Drummond realized that it had all been useless. He was exactly where he had been half an hour before, with the vital difference that the events of the last half-hour could not be repeated. He was caught: it was the finish. Somehow or other the poor girl must have blundered right into the car, and probably asked the occupants for help. She wouldn't have known who they were; she'd just stopped the car on spec, and ... He shook his fists impotently, and at that moment he heard a loud, powerful voice which he recognized at once speaking from the direction of the house.

"Unless Captain Drummond comes into the house within five minutes, I shall personally kill Mrs. Drummond."

And the voice was the voice of Carl Peterson.

17

In which a murderer is murdered at Maybrick Hall

"You appear to have a wonderful faculty for remaining alive, my young friend," remarked Peterson two minutes later, gazing benevolently at Drummond over his clerical collar.

"Principally, Theo, my pet, because you've got such a wonderful faculty for making bloomers," answered Drummond affably.

No trace of the impotent rage he had given way to in the garden showed in his face as he spoke; and yet, in all conscience, the situation was desperate enough. He was unarmed—his revolver had been removed from him as he entered the house—and behind his chair stood two men, each with the muzzle of a gun an inch off his neck. In another corner sat Phyllis, and behind her stood an armed man also. Every now and then his eyes stole round to her, and once he smiled reassuringly—an assurance he was far from feeling. But principally his eyes were fixed on the three men who were sitting at the table opposite him. In the centre was Carl Peterson, smoking the inevitable cigar; and, one on each side of him, sat Count Zadowa and the red-headed Russian Yulowski.

"You can't imagine the pleasant surprise it gave me," Peterson continued gently, "when your charming wife hailed my car. So unexpected: so delightful. And when I realized that you were running about in our grounds here instead of being drowned as that fool No. 10 told me over the telephone.... By the way, where is No. 10."

He turned snarling on the Russian, but it was one of the men behind Drummond's chair who answered.

"He's dead. This guy threw him on the live wires."

"Is that little Franz?" murmured Hugh Drummond, lighting a cigarette. "Yes—I regret to state that he and I had words, and my impression is that he has passed away. Do you mind standing a little further away?" he continued, addressing the men behind him. "You're tickling the back of my neck, and it makes me go all goosey."

"Do you mean to say," said the Russian in his harsh voice, "that it was you and only you outside there?"

"You have guessed it, Adolph," answered Drummond, speaking mechanically. It had seemed to him, suddenly, that, unseen by the others, Phyllis was trying to convey some message. "Alone I did it, to say nothing of that squib-faced bird upstairs with the long arms. In fact, without wishing to exaggerate, I think the total bag is five—with dear old *pericoloso spargersi* as an 'also ran.'"

What was she trying to make him understand.

And then suddenly she began to laugh hysterically, and he half rose from his seat, only to sit down again abruptly as he felt the cold ring of a revolver pressed into the nape of his neck.

"Three and two make five," said Phyllis, half laughing and half crying, "and one makes six. I worked it out to-night, and it all came right."

She went on aimlessly for a while in the same strain, till the Russian swung round on her with a snarl, and told her to shut her mouth. He was talking in low tones to Peterson, and, with one searching look at Hugh, she relapsed into silence. There was no hysteria in that look, and his heart began to pound suddenly in his excitement. For 3256 Mayfair was the number of Peter Darrell's telephone, and she could only mean one thing—that she had got through to Peter before she stopped the car. And if that was so there was still hope, if only he could gain time. Time was the essential factor: time he must have somehow. And how was he to get it? Not by the quiver of an eyelid did the expression on his face change: he still smoked placidly on, looking with resigned boredom at the three men who were now conferring earnestly together. But his mind was racing madly, as he turned things over this way and that. Time: he must gain time.

If his supposition was right, Carl Peterson was in ignorance of the fact that a message had been got through. And in that lay the only chance. Just as in Bridge there comes a time when to win the game one must place a certain card with one of the opponents and play accordingly—so that card must be placed in Peterson's hand. If the placing has been done correctly you take your only chance of winning: if the placing is wrong you lose anyway. And so, starting with that as a foundation, he tried to work out the play of the hand. Peter Darrell knew, and Peterson was in ignorance of the fact.

First—how long did he want? Two hours at least: three if possible. To round up all the gang and get cars in the middle of the night would take time—two hours at the very least. Secondly—and there was the crux—how was he going to get such a respite? For this time he could not hope for another mistake. It was the end, and he knew it.

No trace of mercy showed in the faces of the three men opposite him. He caught occasional remarks, and after a while he realized what the matter under discussion was. Evidently the red-headed Russian was in favour of killing him violently, and at once—and it was Count Zadowa who was advocating caution, while Peterson sat between them listening impassively, with his, eyes fixed on Drummond.

"Bayonet the pair of them," snarled Yulowski at length, as if tired of arguing the point. "I'll do the job if you're too squeamish, and will bury 'em both with the rest of the bodies in the grounds somewhere. Who's to know: who's to find out?"

But Count Zadowa shook his head vigorously.

"That's just where you're wrong, my friend. No one would see you do it more willingly than I—but you've got to remember the rest of his gang."

His voice died away to a whisper, and Drummond could only catch disjointed fragments.

"I know the Black Gang," Zadowa was saying. "You don't. And they know me." Then he heard the word "accident" repeated several times, and at length Yulowski shrugged his shoulders and leaned back in his chair.

"Have it your own way," he remarked. "I don't care how they're killed, as long as they are killed. If you think it's necessary to pretend there has been an accident, we'll have an accident. The only point is what sort of an accident."

But Count Zadowa had apparently not got as far as that, and relapsed into silence. His powers of imagination were not sufficiently great to supply the necessary details, and it was left to Carl Peterson to decide matters.

"Nothing is easier," he remarked suavely, and his eyes were still fixed on Drummond. "We are discussing, my young friend," he continued, raising his voice slightly, "the best way of getting rid of you and your charming wife. I regret that she must share your fate, but I see no way out of it. To keep her permanently about the premises would be too great an inconvenience; and since we can't let her go without involving ourselves in unpleasant notoriety, I fear—as I said—that she must join you. My friend Yulowski wishes to bayonet you both, and bury you in the grounds. He has done a lot of that sort of thing in his time, and I believe I am right in stating that his hand has not lost its cunning since leaving Russia. A little out of practice, perhaps, but the result is the same. On the other hand Count Zadowa, whom you know of old, quite rightly points out that there are the members of your ridiculous gang, who know about him, and might very easily find out about me. And when in a few days your motor-car is hoisted out of the water, and is traced by the registration number as being yours, he fears that not only may he find things very awkward, but that a certain amount of unenviable and undesirable limelight may be thrown on this part of the country, and incidentally on this house. You follow our difficulties so far?"

"With the utmost clarity, Theo," answered Drummond pleasantly.

"It's always such a pleasure talking to you," continued Peterson. "You're so unexpectedly quick on the uptake. Well then—to proceed. Though it will not interfere with me personally—as I leave England in four hours—it will interfere considerably with my plans if the police come poking their noses into this house. We like to hide our light under a bushel, Captain Drummond: we prefer to do our little bit unnoticed. So I feel sure that you will be only too ready to help us in any way you can, and fall in with my suggestion for your decease with goodwill. I have a very warm regard for you in so many ways, and I should hate to think that there was any bad blood between us at the end."

"Carl—my pet—you'll make me cry in a minute," said Drummond quietly. To all outward appearances he was in the same mocking vein as his principal enemy, but a little pulse was beginning to hammer in his throat, and his mouth felt strangely dry. He knew he was being played with as a mouse is played with by a cat, and it was all he could do to stop himself from demanding outright to know what was coming. Out of the corner of his eye he could see Phyllis sitting very white and still, but he didn't dare to look at her direct for fear he might break down. And then, still in the same tone, Peterson went on:

"I knew I could rely on you to meet me. I shall tell Irma when I see her, and she will be very touched by your kindness, Drummond—very touched. But to come back to the point. As my friend Zadowa most justly observed—we want an accident: a real good *bona fide* accident, which will relieve the world of your presence and will bring no scorching glare of publicity upon this house or any of my *confrères* who remain in England. You may recall that that was my original idea, only you seem in the most extraordinary way to have escaped from being drowned. Still, as far as it goes, we have a very good foundation to build on. Your car—duly perceived by the gentleman of limited intelligence who works the bridge—went over the edge. You were duly perceived in it. Strangely enough, his eyesight must have been defective—or else he was so flustered by your amazing action that he was incapable of noticing everything at such a moment. Because he actually failed to see that your charming wife was seated beside you. In the moment of panic when she realized you had fainted, she leant forward—doubtless to try and throw out the clutch. Yes"—his eyes, cold and expressionless, were turned momentarily on Phyllis—"I think that is what she must have done. That accounts for the not very intelligent gate-opener failing to see her. But that she was there is certain. Because, Captain Drummond, both bodies will be recovered from the river the day after to-morrow, shall we say? some two or three miles down-stream."

"Your efforts at drowning have not been vastly successful up to date, Carl, have they?" said Drummond genially. "Do I understand that we are both to be taken out and held under the water, or are you going to use the bath here? That is to say"—and he glanced pointedly at Yulowski—"if such a commodity exists. Or are you again going to experiment with that dope of yours?"

"Wrong on all counts," answered Peterson. "You are far too large and strong, my dear Drummond, to be drowned by such rudimentary methods. And it is more than likely that even if we attempted to do it, the fact that you struggled would be revealed in a post-mortem examination. And that would spoil everything, wouldn't it? No longer would it appear to be an accident: Count Zadowa's masterly arguments would all have been wasted. Why—I might as well agree at once to Yulowski's suggestion of the bayonet. Pray give me credit, my dear young friend, for a little more brains than that."

"I do, Theo: I assure you I do," said Drummond earnestly. "It's only my terrible fear that you'll again go and make a hash of it that inspires my remarks."

"Thank you a thousand times," murmured the clergyman gently. He was leaning forward, his elbows on the table—and for the first time Drummond understood something of the diabolical hatred which Peterson felt for him. He had never shown it before: he was far too big a man ever to betray his feeling unnecessarily. But now, as he sat facing him gently rubbing his big white hands together, Drummond understood.

"Thank you a thousand times," he repeated in the same gentle voice. "And since you are so concerned about the matter, I will tell you my plan in some detail. I need hardly say that any suggestions you make on any points that may strike you will receive my most careful attention. When the car crashed into the water it carried you and your wife with it. We have got as far as that, haven't we? As it plunged downwards you—still unconscious from your dreadful and sudden fainting fit—were hurled out. Your wife, in a magnificent endeavour to save you, rose in her seat and was hurled out too. I think we can safely say that, don't you, seeing that the not too intelligent gatekeeper could not have seen the car as it fell?"

"Go on," said Drummond quietly.

"Interested, I hope," murmured Peterson. "But don't hesitate to stop me if anything is at all obscure. I feel that you have a perfect right to suggest any small alterations you like. Well—to proceed. You were both hurled out as the car plunged into the water, and somewhat naturally you were both thrown forward. Head foremost, you will note, Drummond, you left the car—and your heads struck the stonework of the opposite pier with sickening force, just before you reached the water. In fact, a marked feature of the case, when this dreadful accident is reported in the papers, will be the force with which you both struck that pier. Your two heads were terribly battered. In fact, I have but little doubt that the coroner will decide, when your bodies are recovered some few miles downstream—that you were not in reality drowned, but that the terrific impact on the stone pier killed you instantly. Do you think it's sound up to date?"

"I think it's damned unsound," remarked Drummond languidly. "If you propose to take me and endeavour to make my head impinge on a stone wall, someone is going to get a thick ear. Besides, the bridge isn't open, and even your pal, the not too intelligent gate-keeper, might stick in his toes a bit. Of course"—he added hopefully—"you might say you were doing it for the movies. Tell him you're Charlie Chaplin, but that you dressed in such a hurry you've forgotten your moustache."

The red-headed Russian was snarling venomously.

"Let me get at him, chief. He won't try being funny again."

"No. I shall be too occupied sprinkling myself with insect powder," retorted Drummond vulgarly. "Why, you lousy brute, if you got at me, as you call it, and there wasn't half a battalion of infantry holding guns to my head, I'd break your neck with one hand strapped behind my back."

The Russian half rose to his feet, his teeth bared, and Peterson pulled him back into his chair.

"You'll get your chance in a moment or two, Yulowski," he remarked savagely. Then he turned once more on Drummond, and the genial look had vanished from his face. "Doubtless your humour appeals to some people; it does not to me. Moreover, I am rather in a hurry. I do not propose, Captain Drummond, to take you to the bridge and endeavour to make your head impinge on a wall, as you call it. There is another far simpler method of producing the same result. The impinging will take place in this house. As a soldier you should know the result of a blow over the head with the butt of a rifle. And I can assure you that there will be no bungling this time. Yulowski is an expert in such matters, and I shall stay personally to see that it is done. I think we can give a very creditable imitation of what would have happened had my little story been true, and to-morrow night—I see that it is getting a little too light now for the purpose—your two bodies will be carried over and dropped in the river. The length of time you will both have been dead will be quite correct, within an hour or so—and everything will be most satisfactory for all concerned."

Drummond passed his tongue over his lips, and despite himself his voice shook a little.

"Am I to understand," he said after a moment, "that you propose to let that man butcher us here—in this house—with a rifle?"

"Just so," answered Peterson. "That is exactly what you are to understand."

"You are going to let him bash my wife over the head with a rifle butt?"

"I am going to order him to do so," said Peterson mildly. "And very shortly at that. We must not have any mistakes over the length of time you've both been dead. I confess it sounds drastic, but I can assure you it will be quite sudden. Yulowski, as I told you, is an expert. He had a lot of experience in Russia."

"You inhuman devil!" muttered Drummond dazedly. "You can do what you like to me, but for Heaven's sake let her off."

He was staring fascinated at the Russian, who had risen and crossed to a cupboard in the wall. There was something almost maniacal in the look on his face—the look of a savage, brute beast, confronted with the prey it desires.

"Impossible, my dear young friend," murmured Peterson regretfully. "It affords me no pleasure to have her killed, but I have no alternative. To see you dead, I would cross two continents," he snarled suddenly, "but"—and his voice became normal again—"only bitter necessity compels me to adopt such measures with Phyllis. You see she knows too much." He whispered in Count Zadowa's ear, who rose and left the room, to return shortly with half a dozen more men.

"Yes, she knows too much, and so I fear I cannot let her off. She would be able to tell such a lot of most inconvenient things to the police. This house is so admirably adapted for certain of our activities that it would be a world of pities to draw undesirable attention to it. Especially now that Count Zadowa has been compelled to leave his own office, owing entirely to your reprehensible curiosity."

But Drummond was paying no attention to him. His eyes were fixed on the Russian, who had come back slowly into the centre of the room, carrying a rifle in his hand. It was an ordinary Russian service rifle, and a bayonet was fixed in position. Yulowski handled it lovingly, as he stood beside Peterson—and suddenly Count Zadowa turned white and began to tremble. To throw a bomb into a room and run for your life is one thing: to sit at a table in cold blood and witness a double execution is another. Even Peterson's iron nerves seemed a little shaken, and his hand trembled as he removed his cigar. But there was no sign of relenting on his face; no sign of faltering in his voice as he spoke to the men who had just come into the room.

"In the interest of us all," he remarked steadily, "I have decided that it is necessary to kill both the prisoners." He made a sign, and Drummond, sitting almost paralyzed in his chair, found both his arms gripped, with three men hanging on to each.

"The man," continued Peterson, "has been interfering with our work in England—the work of the Red International. He is the leader of the Black Gang, as you probably know; and as you probably do not know, it is he and his gang who have been responsible for the mysterious disappearance of some of our most trusted workers. Therefore with regard to him there can be no second thought: he deserves death, and he must die. With regard to the woman, the case is a little different. She has done us no active harm—but she is a member of the bourgeois class, and she is his wife. Moreover she knows too much. And so it becomes necessary that she should die too. The reason why I am adopting this method of putting them both out of the way, is—as I have already explained to all save you new-comers—that, when the bodies are discovered, the cause of death will appear to be accidental. They will both of them seem to the police to have gone over the edge of the bridge in the car, and hit their heads on the pier opposite. And to-morrow night you will carry the bodies to the river and drop them in. And that"—he resumed his cigar—"I think is all."

Yulowski handled his rifle lovingly, and once again his teeth showed in a wolfish grin.

"Which shall I take first, chief?" he said carelessly.

"The point is immaterial," returned Peterson. "I think perhaps the woman."

Drummond tried to speak and failed. His tongue was clinging to the roof of his mouth: everything in the room was dancing before his eyes. Dimly he saw the red-headed brute Yulowski swinging his rifle to test it: dimly he saw Phyllis sitting bolt upright, with a calm scornful expression on her face, while two men held her by the arms so that she could not move. And suddenly he croaked horribly.

Then he saw Yulowski put down the rifle and listen intently for a moment.

"What's the matter?" snapped Peterson irritably.

"Do you hear the different note to that dynamo?" said Yulowski.

"What the hell's that got to do with it?" roared Peterson. "Get on with it, damn you—and attend to the dynamo afterwards."

Yulowski nodded, and picked up his rifle again.

"The last time," he said, turning on Drummond with a dreadful look of evil in his face, "that this rifle was used by me was in a cellar in Russia—on even more exalted people than you. I brought it specially with me as a memento, never thinking I should have the pleasure of using it again."

He swung it over his head, and Drummond shut his eyes—to open them again a moment later, as the door flung open and a man distraught with terror dashed in.

"The Black Gang!" he shouted wildly. "Hundreds of them—all round the house. They've cut the wires."

With a fearful curse Peterson leaped to his feet, and the men holding Drummond, dumbfounded at the sudden turning of the tables, let go of his arms. Yulowski stood staring foolishly at the door, and what happened then was so quick that none of the stupefied onlookers raised a finger to prevent it.

With the howl of an enraged beast, Drummond hurled himself on the Russian—blind mad with fury. And when two seconds later a dozen black-cowled, black-hooded figures came swarming in through the door, for one instant they paused in sheer horror.

Pinned to the wall with his own bayonet, which stuck out six inches beyond his back was a red-headed, red-bearded man gibbering horribly in a strange language; whilst creeping towards a benevolent-looking clergyman, who crouched in a corner, was a man they scarce recognized as their leader, so appalling was the look of malignant fury on his face.

Carl Peterson was no coward. In the world in which he moved, there were many strange stories told of his iron nerve and his complete disregard of danger. Moreover Nature had endowed him with physical strength far above the average. But now, for perhaps the first time in his life, he knew the meaning of stark, abject terror.

The sinister men in black—members of that very gang he had come over to England to destroy—seemed to fill the room. Silently, as if they had been drilled to it, they disarmed everyone: then they stood round the walls—waiting. No one spoke: only the horrible imprecations of the dying Russian broke the silence, as he strove feebly to pull out the rifle and bayonet from his chest, which had fixed him to the wall as a dead butterfly is fixed in a collection with a pin.

Peterson had a fleeting vision of a girl with white face and wide, staring eyes beside whom were standing two of the motionless black figures as guards—the girl whom he had just sentenced to a dreadful and horrible death, and then his eyes came back again as if fascinated to the man who was coming towards him. He tried to shrink back further into his corner, plucking with nerveless fingers at his clerical collar—while the sweat poured off his face in a stream. For there was no mercy in Hugh Drummond's eyes: no mercy in the great arms that hung loosely forward. And Peterson realized he deserved none.

And then it came. No word was spoken—Drummond was beyond speech. His hands shot out and Peterson felt himself drawn relentlessly towards the man he had planned to kill, not two minutes before. It was his turn now to wonder desperately if it was some hideous nightmare, even while he struggled impotently in his final frenzy with a man whose strength seemed equal to the strength of ten. He was choking: the grip on his throat was not human in its ferocity. There was a great roaring in his ears, and suddenly he ceased to struggle. The glare in Drummond's eyes hypnotized him, and for the only time in his life he gave up hope.

The room was spinning round: the silent black figures, the dying Yulowski, the girl—all seemed merged in one vast jumble of colour growing darker and darker, out of which one thing and one thing only stood out clear and distinct on his dying consciousness—the blazing eyes of the man who was throttling him. And then, as he felt himself sinking into utter blackness, some dim sense less paralyzed than the rest seemed to tell him that a change had taken place in the room. Something new had come into that whirling nightmare that spun round him: dimly he heard a voice—loud and agonised—a voice he recognized. It was a woman's voice, and after a while the grip on his throat relaxed. He staggered back against the wall gasping and spluttering, and gradually the room ceased to whirl round—the iron bands ceased to press upon his heart and lungs.

It was Irma who stood there: Irma whose piteous cry had pierced through to his brain: Irma who had caused those awful hands to relax their grip just before it was too late. Little by little everything steadied down: he found he could see again—could hear. He still crouched shaking against the wall, but he had got a respite anyway—a breathing-space. And that was all that mattered for the moment—that and the fact that the madness was gone from Hugh Drummond's eyes.

The black figures were still standing there motionless round the walls; the Russian was lolling forward—dead; Phyllis was lying back in her chair unconscious. But Peterson had eyes for none of these things: Count Zadowa shivering in a corner—the huddled group of his own men standing in the centre of the room he passed by without a glance. It was on Drummond his gaze was fixed: Drummond, who stood facing Irma with an almost dazed expression on his face, whilst she pleaded with him in an agony of supplication.

"He ordered that man to brain my wife with a rifle butt," said Drummond hoarsely. "And yet you ask for mercy."

He passed his hand two or three times over his forehead as Irma once again broke into wild pleadings; then he turned and stared at Peterson. She stopped at last, and still he stared at the gasping clergyman as if making up his mind. And, in truth, that was precisely what he was doing. Like most big men he was slow to anger, but once his temper was roused it did not cool easily. And never before in his life had he been in the grip of such cold, maniacal fury as had held him during the last few minutes. Right from the start had Peterson deceived him: from the very moment when he had entered his sitting-room at the Ritz. He had done his best to murder him, and not content with that he had given orders for Phyllis and him to be butchered in cold blood. If the Black Gang had not arrived—had they been half a minute later—it would have been over. Phyllis—his Phyllis—would have been killed by that arch-devil whom he had skewered to the wall with his own rifle. And as the thought took hold of him, his great fists clenched once more and the madness again gleamed in his eyes. For Peterson was the real culprit: Peterson was the leader. To kill the servant and not the master was unjust.

He swung round on the cowering clergyman and gripped him once again by the throat, shaking him as a terrier shakes a rat. He felt the girl Irma plucking feebly at his arm, but he took no notice. In his mind there was room for no thought save the fixed determination to rid the world for ever of this monstrous blackguard. And still the motionless black figures round the wall gave no sign, even when the girl rushed from one to the other imploring their aid. They knew their leader, and though they knew not what had happened to cause his dreadful rage they trusted him implicitly and utterly. Whether it was lawful or not was beside the point: it was just or Hugh Drummond would not have done it. And so they watched and waited, while Drummond, his face blazing, forced the clergyman to his knees, and the girl Irma sank half-fainting by the table.

But once again Fate was to intervene on Peterson's behalf, through the instrumentality of a woman. And mercifully for him the intervention came from the only woman—from the only human being—who could have influenced Drummond at that moment. It was Phyllis who opened her eyes suddenly, and, half-dazed still with the horror of the last few minutes, gazed round the room. She saw the huddled group of men in the centre: she saw the Russian lolling grotesquely forward supported on his own rifle: she saw the Black Gang silent and motionless like avenging judges round the walls. And then she saw her husband bending Carl Peterson's neck farther and farther back, till at any moment it seemed as if it must crack.

For a second she stared at Hugh's face, and saw on it a look which she had never seen before—a look so terrible, that she gave a sharp convulsive cry.

"Let him go, Hugh: let him go. Don't do it."

Her voice pierced his brain, though for a moment it made no impression on the muscles of his arms. A slightly bewildered look came into his eyes: he felt as a dog must feel who is called off his lawful prey by his master.

Let him go—let Carl Peterson go! That was what Phyllis was asking him to do—Phyllis who had stood at death's door not five minutes before. Let him go! And suddenly the madness faded from his eyes: his hands relaxed their grip, and Carl Peterson slipped unconscious to the floor—unconscious but still breathing. He had let him go, and after a while he stepped back and glanced slowly round the room. His eyes lingered for a moment on the dead Russian, they travelled thoughtfully on along the line of black figures. And gradually a smile began to appear on his face—a smile which broadened into a grin.

"Perfectly sound advice, old thing," he remarked at length. "Straight from the stable. I really believe I'd almost lost my temper."

18

In which the Home Secretary is taught the Fox-trot

It was a week later. In Sir Bryan Johnstone's office two men were seated, the features of one of whom, at any rate, were well known to the public. Sir Bryan encouraged no notoriety: the man in the street passed him by without recognition every time. In fact it is doubtful if many of the general public so much as knew his name. But with his companion it was different: as a member of several successive Cabinets, his face was almost as well known as one or two of the lesser lights in the film industry. And it is safe to say that never in the course of a life devoted to the peculiar vagaries of politics had his face worn such an expression of complete bewilderment.

"But it's incredible, Johnstone," he remarked for the fiftieth time. "Simply incredible."

"Nevertheless, Sir John," returned the other, "it is true. I have absolute indisputable proof of the whole thing. And if you may remember, I have long drawn the Government's attention to the spread of these activities in England."

"Yes, yes, I know," said Sir John Haverton a little testily, "but you have never given us chapter and verse like this before."

"To be perfectly frank with you," answered Sir Bryan, "I didn't realize it fully myself until now. Had it not been for the Black Gang stumbling upon this house in Essex—Maybrick Hall—overpowering the owners and putting me on their track, much of this would never have come to light."

"But who are the members of this Black Gang?" demanded the Cabinet Minister.

Sir Bryan Johnstone gave an enigmatic smile.

"At the moment, perhaps," he murmured, "that point had better remain in abeyance. I may say that in the whole of my official career I have never received such a profound surprise as when I found out who the leader of the gang was. In due course, Sir John, it may be necessary to communicate to you his name; but in the meantime I suggest that we should concentrate on the information he has provided us with, and treat him as anonymous. I think you agree that he has deserved well of his country."

"Damned well," grunted the other, with a smile. "He can have a seat in the Cabinet if this is his usual form."

"I hardly think," returned Sir Bryan, smiling even more enigmatically, "that he would help you very much in your proceedings though he might enliven them."

But the Cabinet Minister was once more engrossed in the report he was holding in his hand.

"Incredible," he muttered again. "Incredible."

"And yet, as I said before—the truth," said the other. "That there is an organized and well-financed conspiracy to preach Bolshevism in England we have known for some time: how well organized it is we did not realize. But as you will see from that paper, there is not a single manufacturing town or city in Great Britain that has not got a branch of the organization installed, which can if need be draw plentifully on funds from headquarters. Where those funds come from is at the present moment doubtful: in my own mind I have no doubt that Russia supplies the greater portion. You have in front of you there, Sir John"—he spoke with sudden passion—"the definite proofs of a gigantic attempt at world revolution on the Russian plan. You have in front of you there the proofs of the appalling spread of the Proletarian Sunday Schools, with their abominable propaganda and their avowed attempt to convert the children who attend them to a creed whose beginning is destruction and whose end is chaotic anarchy. You have in front of you there the definite proofs that 80 per cent. of the men engaged in this plot are not visionaries, swayed by some grandiloquent scheme of world reform—are not martyrs sacrificing their lives for what seems to them the good of the community—but criminals, and in many cases murderers. You have there before you the definite proofs that 80 per cent. of these men think only of one thing—the lining of their own pockets, and to carry out that object they are prepared to utterly destroy sound labour in this and every other country. It's not as difficult as it looks; it's not such a big proposition as it seems. Cancer is a small growth compared to the full body of the victim it kills: the cancer of one man's tongue will kill a crowd of a thousand. We're a free country, Sir John; but the time is coming when freedom as we understood it in the past will have to cease. We can't go on as the cesspit of Europe, sheltering microbes who infect us as soon as they are here. We want disinfecting: we want it badly. And then we want sound teaching, with the best representatives of the employers and the best representatives of the employed as the teachers. Otherwise you'll get this."

With his finger he flicked a paper towards the Cabinet Minister.

"'To teach the children the ideal of Revolution—that should be the primary aim of a Proletarian school.'

"Printed at Maybrick Hall," said Sir Bryan grimly. "And listen to this—a couple of the Ten Proletarian Maxims.

"'Thou shalt demand on behalf of your class the COMPLETE SURRENDER of the CAPITALIST CLASS.'

"And another:

"'Thou shalt teach REVOLUTION, for revolution means the abolition of the present political state, the end of Capitalism.'"

He gave a short laugh.

"That's what they're teaching the children. Destruction: destruction: destruction—and not a syllable devoted to construction. What are they going to put in its place? They don't know—and they don't care—as long as they get paid for the teaching."

Sir John Haverton nodded thoughtfully.

"I must go into all this in detail," he remarked. "But in the meantime you have raised my curiosity most infernally about this Black Gang of yours. I seem to remember some extraordinary manifesto in the paper—something to do with that damned blackguard Latter, wasn't it?"

Sir Bryan leaned back in his chair and lit a cigarette.

"There are one or two gaps I haven't filled in myself at the moment," he answered. "But I can tell you very briefly what led us to our discoveries at that house in Essex of which I spoke to you—Maybrick Hall. About six days ago I received a typewritten communication of a similar type to one or two which I had seen before. A certain defect in the typewriter made it clear that the source was the same, and that source was the leader of the Black Gang. Here is the communication."

He opened a drawer in his desk, and passed a sheet of paper across to the Cabinet Minister.

"If," it ran, "jolly old McIver will take his morning constitutional to Maybrick Hall in Essex, he will find much to interest him in that delightful and rural spot. Many specimens, both dead and alive, will be found there, all in a splendid state of preservation. He will also find a great many interesting devices in the house. Above all, let him be careful of an elderly clergyman of beneficent aspect, whose beauty is only marred by a stiff and somewhat swollen neck, accompanied by a charming lady who answers to the name of Janet. They form the peerless gems of the collection, and were on the point of leaving the country with the enclosed packet which I removed from them for safe keeping. My modesty forbids me to tell an unmarried man like you in what portion of dear Janet's garments this little bag was found, but there's no harm in your guessing."

"What the devil?" spluttered Sir John. "Is it a practical joke?"

"Far from it," answered the other. "Read to the end."

"After McIver has done this little job," Sir John read out, "he might like a trip to the north. There was an uninhabited island off the west coast of Mull, which is uninhabited no longer. He may have everything he finds there, with my love.—The Leader of the Black Gang."

Sir John laid down the paper and stared at the Director of Criminal Investigation.

"Is this the rambling of a partially diseased intellect?" he inquired with mild sarcasm.

"Nothing of the sort," returned the other shortly. "McIver and ten plain-clothes men went immediately to Maybrick Hall. And they found it a very peculiar place. There were some fifteen men there—trussed up like so many fowls, and alive. They were laid out in a row in the hall.

"Enthroned in state, in two chairs at the end, and also trussed hand and foot, were the beneficent clergyman and Miss Janet. So much for the living ones, with the exception of an Italian, who was found peacefully sleeping upstairs, with his right wrist padlocked to the wall by a long chain. I've mentioned him last, because he was destined to play a very important part in the matter." He frowned suddenly. "A very important part, confound him," he repeated. "However, we will now pass to the other specimens. In the grounds were discovered—a dead fowl, a dead fox, a dead hound the size of a calf—and three dead men."

Sir John ejaculated explosively, sitting up in his chair.

"They had all died from the same cause," continued the other imperturbably, "electrocution. But that was nothing compared to what they found inside. In an upstair room was a dreadful-looking specimen more like an ape than a man, whose neck was broken. In addition, the main artery of his left arm had been severed with a knife. And even that was mild to what they found downstairs. Supported against the wall was a red-headed man stone dead. A bayonet fixed to a rifle had been driven clean through his chest, and stuck six inches into the wall behind him. And on that the body was supported."

"Good heavens!" said Sir John, aghast. "Who had done it?"

"The leader of the Black Gang had done it all, fighting desperately for his own life and that of his wife. One of the men lashed up in the hall turned King's Evidence and told us everything. I'm not going to weary you with the entire story, because you wouldn't believe it. This man had heard everything: had been present through it all. He heard how this leader—a man of gigantic strength—had thrown his wife over the high live-wire fence, just as the hound was on top of them, and the hound dashing after her had electrocuted itself. He heard how the girl, rushing blindly through the night in an unknown country, had stumbled by luck on the local post office, and managed to get a telephone call through to London, where she found the rest of the gang assembled and waiting—their suspicions aroused over some message received that evening from the Ritz. Then she left the post office and was wandering aimlessly along the road, when a car pulled up suddenly in front of her. Inside was a clergyman accompanied by another man—neither of whom she recognized. They offered her a lift, and the next thing she knew was that she'd been trapped again, and was back at Maybrick Hall. So much this man heard: the rest he saw. The leader of the Black Gang and his wife were sentenced to death by the clergyman.... Clergyman!" Sir Bryan shook his fist in the air. "I'd give a year's screw to have laid my hands on that clergyman."

"He escaped?" cried the other.

"All in due course," said Sir Bryan. "They were sentenced to death by having their brains bashed out with the butt of a rifle—after which they were to be thrown in the river. It was to be made to appear an accident. And the man who was to do it was a Russian called Yulowski—one of the men who butchered the Russian Royal family.... A devil of the most inhuman description. He literally had the rifle raised to kill the girl, when the Black Gang, having cut the wire fence, arrived in the nick of time. And it was then that the leader of that gang, who had thought he was on the point of seeing his wife's brains dashed out, took advantage of the utter confusion and sprang on the Russian with a roar of rage. The man who told us stated that he had never dreamed such a blow was possible as the rifle thrust which pierced clean through the Russian. It split him like a rotten cabbage, and he died in three minutes."

"But, my dear fellow," spluttered the Cabinet Minister, "you can't expect me to believe all this. You're pulling my leg."

"Never further from it in my life, Haverton," said the other. "I admit it seems a bit over the odds, but every word I've told you is gospel. To return to the discoveries. McIver found that the house was the headquarters of a vast criminal organization. There were schemes of the most fantastic description cut and dried in every detail. Some of them were stupid: some were not. I have them all here. This one"—he glanced through some papers on his desk—"concerns the blowing of a large gap in one of the retaining walls of the big reservoir at Staines. This one concerns a perfectly-thought-out plot on your life when you go to Beauchamp Hall next week. You were to be found dead in your railway carriage."

"What!" roared Sir John, springing to his feet.

"It would very likely have failed," said Sir Bryan calmly, "but they would have tried again. They don't like you or your views at all—these gentlemen. But those are the least important. From time immemorial wild, fanatical youths have done similar things: the danger was far greater and more subtle. And perhaps the most dangerous activity of all was what I have spoken about already—Maybrick Hall was the headquarters of these poisonous Proletarian Sunday Schools. But in addition to that there was forgery going on there on a big scale: money is necessary for their activities. There were also long lists of their agents in different parts of the country, and detailed instructions for fomenting industrial unrest. But you have it all there—you can read it at your leisure for yourself. Particularly I commend to your notice the series of pamphlets on Ireland, and the methods suggested for promoting discord between England and France, and England and America."

Sir Bryan lit a cigarette.

"To return to the personal side of it. McIver, engrossed in his search, paid very little attention to the row of mummies in the hall. They certainly seemed extraordinarily safe, and one can hardly blame him. But the fact remains that, at some period during the morning, the Italian, who, if you remember, was padlocked in a bedroom upstairs, escaped. How, I can't tell you: he must have had a key in his pocket. They found the padlock open, and the room empty. And going downstairs they found the chairs recently occupied by the clergyman and Miss Janet empty also. Moreover from that moment no trace of any of them has been found. It is as if the earth had opened and swallowed them. Which brings us to the packet enclosed with the letter from the leader of the Black Gang."

He crossed to a safe and took out the little chamois leather bag of diamonds.

"Nice stones," he remarked quietly. "Worth literally a King's ransom. The pink one is part of the Russian crown jewels: the remainder belonged to the Grand Duke Georgius, who was murdered by the Bolshevists. His son, who had these in his possession, died ten days ago of an overdose of a sleeping-draught in Amsterdam. At least that is what I understood until I received these. Now I am not so sure. I would go further, and say I am quite sure that even if he did die of an overdose, it was administered by someone else. And it was administered by the beneficent clergyman calling himself the Reverend Theodosius Longmoor—the most amazing international criminal of this or any other age—the man who, with Miss Janet and the Italian, has vanished into thin air, right under McIver's nose."

"And you mean to say that this man has been in England and you haven't laid him by the heels?" said Sir John incredulously.

"Unfortunately that is what I mean," answered the other. "The police of four continents know about him, but that's a very different thing from proof. This time we had proof—these diamonds: and the man has vanished—utterly and completely. He is the master mind who controls and directs, but very rarely actually does anything himself. That's why he's so devilishly difficult to catch. But we'll do it sooner or later."

The Cabinet Minister was once more studying the typewritten communication from the leader of the Black Gang.

"It's the most astounding affair, this, Johnstone," he said at length. "Most astounding. And what's all this about the island off the coast of Mull?"

Sir Bryan laughed.

"Not the least astounding part of the whole show, I assure you. But for you to understand it better I must go back two or three months, to the time when we first became aware of the existence of the Black Gang. A series of very strange disappearances were taking place: men were being spirited away, without leaving a trace behind them. Of course we knew about it, but in view of the fact that our assistance was never asked to find them, and still more in view of the fact that in every case they were people whose room we preferred to their company, we lay low and said nothing.

"From unofficial inquiries I had carried out we came to the conclusion that this mysterious Black Gang was a reality, and that, further, it was intimately connected with these disappearances. But we also came to the conclusion that the ideals and objects of this gang were in every way desirable. Such a thing, of course, could not be admitted officially: the abduction of anyone is a criminal offence. But we came to the conclusion that the Black Gang was undoubtedly an extremely powerful and ably led organization whose object was simply and solely to fight the Red element in England. The means they adopted were undoubtedly illegal—but the results were excellent. Whenever a man appeared preaching Bolshevism, after a few days he simply disappeared. In short, a reign of terror was established amongst the terrorists. And it was to put that right, I have no doubt, that the Reverend Theodosius Longmoor arrived in this country."

Sir Bryan thoughtfully lit another cigarette.

"To return to the island. McIver went there, and after some little difficulty located it, out of the twenty or thirty to which the description might apply. He found it far from uninhabited, just as that letter says. He found it occupied by some fifty or sixty rabid anarchists—the gentlemen who had so mysteriously disappeared—who were presided over by twenty large demobilized soldiers commanded by an ex-sergeant-major of the Guards. The sixty frenzied anarchists, he gathered, were running a state on communist lines, as interpreted by the ex-sergeant-major. And the interpretation moved even McIver to tears of laughter. It appeared that once every three hours they were all drawn up in a row, and the sergeant-major, with a voice like a bull, would bellow:

"'Should the ruling classes have money?'

"Then they answered in unison—'No.'

"'Should anyone have money?' Again they answered 'No.'

"'Should everyone work for the common good for love?' 'Yes.'

"Whereat he would roar: 'Well, in this 'ere island there ain't no ruling classes, and there ain't no money, and there's dam' little love, so go and plant more potatoes, you lop-eared sons of Beelzebub.'

"At which point the parade broke up in disorder."

Sir John was shaking helplessly.

"This is a jest, Johnstone. You're joking."

"I'm not," answered the other. "But I think you'll admit that the man who started the whole show—the leader of the Black Gang—is a humorist, to put it mildly, who cannot well be spared."

"My dear fellow, as I said before, the Cabinet is the only place for him. If only he'd export two or three of my colleagues to this island and let 'em plant potatoes I'd take off my hat to him. Tell me—do I know him?"

Sir Bryan smiled.

"I'm not certain: you may. But the point, Haverton, is this. We must take cognizance of the whole thing, if we acknowledge it at all. Therefore shall we assume that everything I have been telling you is a fairy story: that the Black Gang is non-existent—I may say that it will be shortly—and that what has already appeared in the papers is just a hoax by some irresponsible person? Unless we do that there will be a *cause célèbre* fought out on class prejudice—a most injudicious thing at the present moment. I may say that the island is shut down, and the sixty pioneers have departed to other countries. Also quite a number of those agents whose names are on the list you have, have left our shores during the past few days. It is merely up to us to see that they don't come back. But nothing has come out in the papers: and I don't want anything to come out either."

He paused suddenly, as a cheerful voice was heard in the office outside.

"Ah! here is one Captain Drummond, whom I asked to come round this morning," he continued, with a faint smile. "I wonder if you know him."

"Drummond?" repeated the other. "Is he a vast fellow with an ugly face?"

"That's the man," said Sir Bryan.

"I've seen him at his aunt's—old Lady Meltrose. She says he's the biggest fool in London."

Sir Bryan's smile grew more pronounced as the door opened and Hugh came in.

"Morning, Tum-tum," he boomed genially. "How's the liver and all that?"

"Morning, Hugh. Do you know Sir John Haverton?"

"Morning, Sir John. Jolly old Cabinet merry and bright? Or did you all go down on Purple Polly at Goodwood yesterday?"

Sir John rose a little grimly.

"We have other things to do besides backing horses, Captain Drummond. I think we have met at Lady Meltrose's house, haven't we?"

"More than likely," said Hugh affably. "I don't often dine there: she ropes in such a ghastly crowd of bores, don't you know."

"I feel sure, Captain Drummond, that you're an admirable judge." Sir John turned to Sir Bryan Johnstone and held out his hand. "Well, I must be off. Good-morning, Johnstone—and you've thoroughly roused my curiosity. I'd very much like to know who the gentleman is whom we've been discussing. And in the meantime I'll look through these papers and let you know my decision in due course."

He bustled out of the office, and Hugh sank into a chair with a sigh of relief.

"The old boy's clothes seem full of body this morning, Tum-tum," he remarked as the door closed. "Indigestion—or don't the elastic-sided boots fit?"

"Do you know what we have been discussing, Hugh?" said the other quietly.

"Not an earthly, old man. Was it that new one about the girl in the grocer's shop?"

"We've been discussing the leader of the Black Gang," said Sir Bryan, with his eyes fixed on the man sprawling in the chair opposite.

Not by the twitch of a muscle did Drummond's face change: he seemed engrossed in the task of selecting a cigarette.

"You've been in Deauville, haven't you, Hugh—the last few days?"

"Quite right, old man. All among the fairies."

"You don't know that a burglary has taken place at your house in London?"

"A burglary!" Drummond sat up with a jerk. "Why the deuce hasn't Denny told me?"

"A very small one," said Sir Bryan, "committed by myself, and perhaps he doesn't know. I took—your typewriter."

For a few moments Hugh Drummond stared at him in silence: then his lips began to twitch.

"I see," he said at length. "I meant to have that defective 's' repaired."

"You took me in, old boy," continued Sir Bryan, "utterly and absolutely. If it hadn't been for one of the men at Maybrick Hall turning King's evidence, I don't believe I should have found out now."

"Well, what are you going to do about it?" asked Drummond after a pause.

"Nothing. I was discussing the matter with Sir John this morning, and we both agreed that you either deserved penal servitude or a seat in the Cabinet. And since neither course commends itself to us, we have decided to do nothing. There are reasons, which you will appreciate, against any publicity at the moment. But, Hugh, the Black Gang must cease."

Drummond nodded.

"Carried, *nem. con.*, Tum-tum. It shall automatically dissolve to-day."

"And further," continued Sir Bryan, "will you relieve my curiosity and tell me what sent Charles Latter mad?"

"I did," said Drummond grimly, "as I told that ass McIver over a cocktail at the Regency. He was plotting to blow up three thousand men's employment, Tum-tum, with gun-cotton. It was at his instigation that four men were killed in Manchester as the result of another outrage. So I lashed him to his bed, and underneath him I put what he thought was a slab of gun-cotton with fuse attached. It wasn't gun-cotton: it was wood. And he went mad." He paused for a moment, and then continued. "Now one for you. Why did you let Carl Peterson escape? I nearly killed him that night, after I'd bayoneted the Russian."

"How did you know he had escaped?" demanded Sir Bryan.

Hugh felt in his pocket and produced a note. "Read it," he said, passing it across the desk.

"It was a pity you forgot that there might be another key to the padlock, Captain Drummond," it ran. "And Giuseppi is an old friend of mine. I quite enjoyed our single."

Sir Bryan returned the note without a word, and Drummond replaced it in his pocket.

"That's twice," he said quietly, and suddenly the Director of Criminal Investigation, than whom no shrewder judge of men lived, saw and understood the real Drummond below the surface of inanity—the real Drummond, cool, resourceful, and inflexible of will—the real Drummond who was capable of organizing and carrying through anything and everything once he had set his mind to it.

"That's twice," he repeated, still in the same quiet tone. "Next time—I win."

"But no more Black Gang, Hugh," said the other warningly.

Drummond waved a huge hand. "I have spoken, Tum-tum. A rose by any other name, perhaps—but no more Black Gang."

He rose and grinned at his friend.

"It's deuced good of you, old man, and all that..."

The eyes of the two men met.

"If it was found out, I should be looking for another job," remarked Sir Bryan dryly. "And perhaps I should not get the two thousand pounds which I understand the widow of the late lamented Ginger Martin has received anonymously."

"Shut up," said Drummond awkwardly.

"Delighted, old man," returned the other. "But the police in that district are demanding a rise of pay. She has been drunk and disorderly five times in the last week."

*****

To those strong-minded individuals who habitually read the entrancing chit-chat of Mrs. Tattle in *The Daily Observer*, there appeared the following morning a delightful description of the last big fancy-dress ball of the season held at the Albert Hall the preceding night. Much of it may be passed over as unworthy of perpetuation, but the concluding paragraph had its points of interest.

"Half way through the evening," she wrote in her breezy way, "just as I was consuming an ice in one hand with the Duchess of Sussex, and nibbling the last of the asparagus in the other with the Princess of Montevideo, tastefully disguised as an umbrella stand, we were treated to the thrill of the evening. It seemed as if suddenly there sprang up all round the room a mass of mysterious figures clothed from head to foot in black. The dear Princess grew quite hysterical, and began to wonder if it was a 'hold up' as she so graphically described it. In fact, for safety, she secreted the glass-headed parasol—the only remaining heirloom of the Royal House—and which formed a prominent part of her costume, behind a neighbouring palm. Whispers of the mysterious Black Gang were heard on all sides, but we were soon reassured. Belovd'st, they all carried champagne bottles! Wasn't it too, too thrilling!! And after a while they all formed up in a row, and at a word from the leader—a huge man, my dears, puffectly 'uge—they discharged the corks in a volley at one of the boxes, which sheltered no less than two celebrities—Sir Bryan Johnstone, the chief of all the policemen, and Sir John Haverton, the Home Secretary. It is rumoured that one of the corks became embedded in Sir John's right eye—but rumour is a lying jade, is not she? Anyway loud sounds of revelry and mirth were heard proceeding from the box, and going a little later to powder my nose I distinctly

151

saw Sir John being taught the intricacies of the fox-trot by the huge man in the passage. Presumably the cork had by then been removed from his eye, but one never knows, does one? Anything can happen at an Albert Hall ball, especially at the end of the season."

Printed in Great Britain
by Amazon